I0308942

C-2709 CAREER EXAMINATION SERIES

This is your PASSBOOK for...

Senior Administrative Analyst

Test Preparation Study Guide
Questions & Answers

NLC®

NATIONAL LEARNING CORPORATION®

National Learning Corporation

212 Michael Drive, Syosset, NY 11791
(516) 921-8888 • www.passbooks.com
E-mail: info@passbooks.com

PASSBOOK® SERIES

THE *PASSBOOK® SERIES* has been created to prepare applicants and candidates for the ultimate academic battlefield – the examination room.

At some time in our lives, each and every one of us may be required to take an examination – for validation, matriculation, admission, qualification, registration, certification, or licensure.

Based on the assumption that every applicant or candidate has met the basic formal educational standards, has taken the required number of courses, and read the necessary texts, the *PASSBOOK® SERIES* furnishes the one special preparation which may assure passing with confidence, instead of failing with insecurity. Examination questions – together with answers – are furnished as the basic vehicle for study so that the mysteries of the examination and its compounding difficulties may be eliminated or diminished by a sure method.

This book is meant to help you pass your examination provided that you qualify and are serious in your objective.

The entire field is reviewed through the huge store of content information which is succinctly presented through a provocative and challenging approach – the question-and-answer method.

A climate of success is established by furnishing the correct answers at the end of each test.

You soon learn to recognize types of questions, forms of questions, and patterns of questioning. You may even begin to anticipate expected outcomes.

You perceive that many questions are repeated or adapted so that you can gain acute insights, which may enable you to score many sure points.

You learn how to confront new questions, or types of questions, and to attack them confidently and work out the correct answers.

You note objectives and emphases, and recognize pitfalls and dangers, so that you may make positive educational adjustments.

Moreover, you are kept fully informed in relation to new concepts, methods, practices, and directions in the field.

You discover that you are actually taking the examination all the time: you are preparing for the examination by "taking" an examination, not by reading extraneous and/or supererogatory textbooks.

In short, this PASSBOOK®, used directedly, should be an important factor in helping you to pass your test.

SENIOR ADMINISTRATIVE ANALYST

DUTIES

Under general supervision, performs technical work in personnel management. Performs professional work in reviewing budgeting requirements and controls; preparation and conduct of management and administrative surveys; evaluation of organizational structures, policies, programs, projects, and contracts; may supervise subordinate staff; performs related work.

TYPICAL WORK ACTIVITIES

Conducts method and systems studies of departmental and federal program procedures; proposes organizational and procedural recommendations; prepares narrative reports; analyzes budget requests of departments and agencies including capital expenditures; analyzes proposals and prepares grant applications for federally funded programs; conducts feasibility studies and makes subsequent recommenations; works with planning agencies and community groups to encourage their participation in grant programs; conducts research for a variety of special assignments; may supervise and review the work of subordinates.

SCOPE OF THE EXAMINATION:

The written examination will cover knowledges, skills and abilities such as:

1. Administrative analysis;
2. Administrative management and supervision;
3. Budgeting;
4. Understanding and interpreting written material;
5. Understanding and interpreting tabular material; and
6. Preparing written material.

HOW TO TAKE A TEST

I. YOU MUST PASS AN EXAMINATION

A. WHAT EVERY CANDIDATE SHOULD KNOW

Examination applicants often ask us for help in preparing for the written test. What can I study in advance? What kinds of questions will be asked? How will the test be given? How will the papers be graded?

As an applicant for a civil service examination, you may be wondering about some of these things. Our purpose here is to suggest effective methods of advance study and to describe civil service examinations.

Your chances for success on this examination can be increased if you know how to prepare. Those "pre-examination jitters" can be reduced if you know what to expect. You can even experience an adventure in good citizenship if you know why civil service exams are given.

B. WHY ARE CIVIL SERVICE EXAMINATIONS GIVEN?

Civil service examinations are important to you in two ways. As a citizen, you want public jobs filled by employees who know how to do their work. As a job seeker, you want a fair chance to compete for that job on an equal footing with other candidates. The best-known means of accomplishing this two-fold goal is the competitive examination.

Exams are widely publicized throughout the nation. They may be administered for jobs in federal, state, city, municipal, town or village governments or agencies.

Any citizen may apply, with some limitations, such as the age or residence of applicants. Your experience and education may be reviewed to see whether you meet the requirements for the particular examination. When these requirements exist, they are reasonable and applied consistently to all applicants. Thus, a competitive examination may cause you some uneasiness now, but it is your privilege and safeguard.

C. HOW ARE CIVIL SERVICE EXAMS DEVELOPED?

Examinations are carefully written by trained technicians who are specialists in the field known as "psychological measurement," in consultation with recognized authorities in the field of work that the test will cover. These experts recommend the subject matter areas or skills to be tested; only those knowledges or skills important to your success on the job are included. The most reliable books and source materials available are used as references. Together, the experts and technicians judge the difficulty level of the questions.

Test technicians know how to phrase questions so that the problem is clearly stated. Their ethics do not permit "trick" or "catch" questions. Questions may have been tried out on sample groups, or subjected to statistical analysis, to determine their usefulness.

Written tests are often used in combination with performance tests, ratings of training and experience, and oral interviews. All of these measures combine to form the best-known means of finding the right person for the right job.

II. HOW TO PASS THE WRITTEN TEST

A. NATURE OF THE EXAMINATION

To prepare intelligently for civil service examinations, you should know how they differ from school examinations you have taken. In school you were assigned certain definite pages to read or subjects to cover. The examination questions were quite detailed and usually emphasized memory. Civil service exams, on the other hand, try to discover your present ability to perform the duties of a position, plus your potentiality to learn these duties. In other words, a civil service exam attempts to predict how successful you will be. Questions cover such a broad area that they cannot be as minute and detailed as school exam questions.

In the public service similar kinds of work, or positions, are grouped together in one "class." This process is known as *position-classification.* All the positions in a class are paid according to the salary range for that class. One class title covers all of these positions, and they are all tested by the same examination.

B. FOUR BASIC STEPS

1) Study the announcement

How, then, can you know what subjects to study? Our best answer is: "Learn as much as possible about the class of positions for which you've applied." The exam will test the knowledge, skills and abilities needed to do the work.

Your most valuable source of information about the position you want is the official exam announcement. This announcement lists the training and experience qualifications. Check these standards and apply only if you come reasonably close to meeting them.

The brief description of the position in the examination announcement offers some clues to the subjects which will be tested. Think about the job itself. Review the duties in your mind. Can you perform them, or are there some in which you are rusty? Fill in the blank spots in your preparation.

Many jurisdictions preview the written test in the exam announcement by including a section called "Knowledge and Abilities Required," "Scope of the Examination," or some similar heading. Here you will find out specifically what fields will be tested.

2) Review your own background

Once you learn in general what the position is all about, and what you need to know to do the work, ask yourself which subjects you already know fairly well and which need improvement. You may wonder whether to concentrate on improving your strong areas or on building some background in your fields of weakness. When the announcement has specified "some knowledge" or "considerable knowledge," or has used adjectives like "beginning principles of..." or "advanced ... methods," you can get a clue as to the number and difficulty of questions to be asked in any given field. More questions, and hence broader coverage, would be included for those subjects which are more important in the work. Now weigh your strengths and weaknesses against the job requirements and prepare accordingly.

3) Determine the level of the position

Another way to tell how intensively you should prepare is to understand the level of the job for which you are applying. Is it the entering level? In other words, is this the position in which beginners in a field of work are hired? Or is it an intermediate or advanced level? Sometimes this is indicated by such words as "Junior" or "Senior" in the class title. Other jurisdictions use Roman numerals to designate the level – Clerk I, Clerk II, for example. The word "Supervisor" sometimes appears in the title. If the level is not indicated by the title, check the description of duties. Will you be working under very close supervision, or will you have responsibility for independent decisions in this work?

4) Choose appropriate study materials

Now that you know the subjects to be examined and the relative amount of each subject to be covered, you can choose suitable study materials. For beginning level jobs, or even advanced ones, if you have a pronounced weakness in some aspect of your training, read a modern, standard textbook in that field. Be sure it is up to date and has general coverage. Such books are normally available at your library, and the librarian will be glad to help you locate one. For entry-level positions, questions of appropriate difficulty are chosen – neither highly advanced questions, nor those too simple. Such questions require careful thought but not advanced training.

If the position for which you are applying is technical or advanced, you will read more advanced, specialized material. If you are already familiar with the basic principles of your field, elementary textbooks would waste your time. Concentrate on advanced textbooks and technical periodicals. Think through the concepts and review difficult problems in your field.

These are all general sources. You can get more ideas on your own initiative, following these leads. For example, training manuals and publications of the government agency which employs workers in your field can be useful, particularly for technical and professional positions. A letter or visit to the government department involved may result in more specific study suggestions, and certainly will provide you with a more definite idea of the exact nature of the position you are seeking.

III. KINDS OF TESTS

Tests are used for purposes other than measuring knowledge and ability to perform specified duties. For some positions, it is equally important to test ability to make adjustments to new situations or to profit from training. In others, basic mental abilities not dependent on information are essential. Questions which test these things may not appear as pertinent to the duties of the position as those which test for knowledge and information. Yet they are often highly important parts of a fair examination. For very general questions, it is almost impossible to help you direct your study efforts. What we can do is to point out some of the more common of these general abilities needed in public service positions and describe some typical questions.

1) General information

Broad, general information has been found useful for predicting job success in some kinds of work. This is tested in a variety of ways, from vocabulary lists to questions about current events. Basic background in some field of work, such as sociology or economics, may be sampled in a group of questions. Often these are principles which have become familiar to most persons through exposure rather than through formal training. It is difficult to advise you how to study for these questions; being alert to the world around you is our best suggestion.

2) Verbal ability

An example of an ability needed in many positions is verbal or language ability. Verbal ability is, in brief, the ability to use and understand words. Vocabulary and grammar tests are typical measures of this ability. Reading comprehension or paragraph interpretation questions are common in many kinds of civil service tests. You are given a paragraph of written material and asked to find its central meaning.

3) Numerical ability

Number skills can be tested by the familiar arithmetic problem, by checking paired lists of numbers to see which are alike and which are different, or by interpreting charts and graphs. In the latter test, a graph may be printed in the test booklet which you are asked to use as the basis for answering questions.

4) Observation

A popular test for law-enforcement positions is the observation test. A picture is shown to you for several minutes, then taken away. Questions about the picture test your ability to observe both details and larger elements.

5) Following directions

In many positions in the public service, the employee must be able to carry out written instructions dependably and accurately. You may be given a chart with several columns, each column listing a variety of information. The questions require you to carry out directions involving the information given in the chart.

6) Skills and aptitudes

Performance tests effectively measure some manual skills and aptitudes. When the skill is one in which you are trained, such as typing or shorthand, you can practice. These tests are often very much like those given in business school or high school courses. For many of the other skills and aptitudes, however, no short-time preparation can be made. Skills and abilities natural to you or that you have developed throughout your lifetime are being tested.

Many of the general questions just described provide all the data needed to answer the questions and ask you to use your reasoning ability to find the answers. Your best preparation for these tests, as well as for tests of facts and ideas, is to be at your physical and mental best. You, no doubt, have your own methods of getting into an exam-taking mood and keeping "in shape." The next section lists some ideas on this subject.

IV. KINDS OF QUESTIONS

Only rarely is the "essay" question, which you answer in narrative form, used in civil service tests. Civil service tests are usually of the short-answer type. Full instructions for answering these questions will be given to you at the examination. But in case this is your first experience with short-answer questions and separate answer sheets, here is what you need to know:

1) Multiple-choice Questions

Most popular of the short-answer questions is the "multiple choice" or "best answer" question. It can be used, for example, to test for factual knowledge, ability to solve problems or judgment in meeting situations found at work.

A multiple-choice question is normally one of three types—

- It can begin with an incomplete statement followed by several possible endings. You are to find the one ending which *best* completes the statement, although some of the others may not be entirely wrong.
- It can also be a complete statement in the form of a question which is answered by choosing one of the statements listed.

- It can be in the form of a problem – again you select the best answer.

Here is an example of a multiple-choice question with a discussion which should give you some clues as to the method for choosing the right answer:

When an employee has a complaint about his assignment, the action which will *best* help him overcome his difficulty is to
A. discuss his difficulty with his coworkers
B. take the problem to the head of the organization
C. take the problem to the person who gave him the assignment
D. say nothing to anyone about his complaint

In answering this question, you should study each of the choices to find which is best. Consider choice "A" – Certainly an employee may discuss his complaint with fellow employees, but no change or improvement can result, and the complaint remains unresolved. Choice "B" is a poor choice since the head of the organization probably does not know what assignment you have been given, and taking your problem to him is known as "going over the head" of the supervisor. The supervisor, or person who made the assignment, is the person who can clarify it or correct any injustice. Choice "C" is, therefore, correct. To say nothing, as in choice "D," is unwise. Supervisors have and interest in knowing the problems employees are facing, and the employee is seeking a solution to his problem.

2) True/False Questions

The "true/false" or "right/wrong" form of question is sometimes used. Here a complete statement is given. Your job is to decide whether the statement is right or wrong.

SAMPLE: A roaming cell-phone call to a nearby city costs less than a non-roaming call to a distant city.

This statement is wrong, or false, since roaming calls are more expensive.

This is not a complete list of all possible question forms, although most of the others are variations of these common types. You will always get complete directions for answering questions. Be sure you understand *how* to mark your answers – ask questions until you do.

V. RECORDING YOUR ANSWERS

Computer terminals are used more and more today for many different kinds of exams.

For an examination with very few applicants, you may be told to record your answers in the test booklet itself. Separate answer sheets are much more common. If this separate answer sheet is to be scored by machine – and this is often the case – it is highly important that you mark your answers correctly in order to get credit.

An electronic scoring machine is often used in civil service offices because of the speed with which papers can be scored. Machine-scored answer sheets must be marked with a pencil, which will be given to you. This pencil has a high graphite content which responds to the electronic scoring machine. As a matter of fact, stray dots may register as answers, so do not let your pencil rest on the answer sheet while you are pondering the correct answer. Also, if your pencil lead breaks or is otherwise defective, ask for another.

Since the answer sheet will be dropped in a slot in the scoring machine, be careful not to bend the corners or get the paper crumpled.

The answer sheet normally has five vertical columns of numbers, with 30 numbers to a column. These numbers correspond to the question numbers in your test booklet. After each number, going across the page are four or five pairs of dotted lines. These short dotted lines have small letters or numbers above them. The first two pairs may also have a "T" or "F" above the letters. This indicates that the first two pairs only are to be used if the questions are of the true-false type. If the questions are multiple choice, disregard the "T" and "F" and pay attention only to the small letters or numbers.

Answer your questions in the manner of the sample that follows:

32. The largest city in the United States is
    - A. Washington, D.C.
    - B. New York City
    - C. Chicago
    - D. Detroit
    - E. San Francisco

1) Choose the answer you think is best. (New York City is the largest, so "B" is correct.)
2) Find the row of dotted lines numbered the same as the question you are answering. (Find row number 32)
3) Find the pair of dotted lines corresponding to the answer. (Find the pair of lines under the mark "B.")
4) Make a solid black mark between the dotted lines.

VI. BEFORE THE TEST

Common sense will help you find procedures to follow to get ready for an examination. Too many of us, however, overlook these sensible measures. Indeed, nervousness and fatigue have been found to be the most serious reasons why applicants fail to do their best on civil service tests. Here is a list of reminders:

- Begin your preparation early – Don't wait until the last minute to go scurrying around for books and materials or to find out what the position is all about.
- Prepare continuously – An hour a night for a week is better than an all-night cram session. This has been definitely established. What is more, a night a week for a month will return better dividends than crowding your study into a shorter period of time.
- Locate the place of the exam – You have been sent a notice telling you when and where to report for the examination. If the location is in a different town or otherwise unfamiliar to you, it would be well to inquire the best route and learn something about the building.
- Relax the night before the test – Allow your mind to rest. Do not study at all that night. Plan some mild recreation or diversion; then go to bed early and get a good night's sleep.
- Get up early enough to make a leisurely trip to the place for the test – This way unforeseen events, traffic snarls, unfamiliar buildings, etc. will not upset you.
- Dress comfortably – A written test is not a fashion show. You will be known by number and not by name, so wear something comfortable.

- Leave excess paraphernalia at home – Shopping bags and odd bundles will get in your way. You need bring only the items mentioned in the official notice you received; usually everything you need is provided. Do not bring reference books to the exam. They will only confuse those last minutes and be taken away from you when in the test room.
- Arrive somewhat ahead of time – If because of transportation schedules you must get there very early, bring a newspaper or magazine to take your mind off yourself while waiting.
- Locate the examination room – When you have found the proper room, you will be directed to the seat or part of the room where you will sit. Sometimes you are given a sheet of instructions to read while you are waiting. Do not fill out any forms until you are told to do so; just read them and be prepared.
- Relax and prepare to listen to the instructions
- If you have any physical problem that may keep you from doing your best, be sure to tell the test administrator. If you are sick or in poor health, you really cannot do your best on the exam. You can come back and take the test some other time.

VII. AT THE TEST

The day of the test is here and you have the test booklet in your hand. The temptation to get going is very strong. Caution! There is more to success than knowing the right answers. You must know how to identify your papers and understand variations in the type of short-answer question used in this particular examination. Follow these suggestions for maximum results from your efforts:

1) Cooperate with the monitor

The test administrator has a duty to create a situation in which you can be as much at ease as possible. He will give instructions, tell you when to begin, check to see that you are marking your answer sheet correctly, and so on. He is not there to guard you, although he will see that your competitors do not take unfair advantage. He wants to help you do your best.

2) Listen to all instructions

Don't jump the gun! Wait until you understand all directions. In most civil service tests you get more time than you need to answer the questions. So don't be in a hurry. Read each word of instructions until you clearly understand the meaning. Study the examples, listen to all announcements and follow directions. Ask questions if you do not understand what to do.

3) Identify your papers

Civil service exams are usually identified by number only. You will be assigned a number; you must not put your name on your test papers. Be sure to copy your number correctly. Since more than one exam may be given, copy your exact examination title.

4) Plan your time

Unless you are told that a test is a "speed" or "rate of work" test, speed itself is usually not important. Time enough to answer all the questions will be provided, but this does not mean that you have all day. An overall time limit has been set. Divide the total time (in minutes) by the number of questions to determine the approximate time you have for each question.

5) Do not linger over difficult questions

If you come across a difficult question, mark it with a paper clip (useful to have along) and come back to it when you have been through the booklet. One caution if you do this – be sure to skip a number on your answer sheet as well. Check often to be sure that you have not lost your place and that you are marking in the row numbered the same as the question you are answering.

6) Read the questions

Be sure you know what the question asks! Many capable people are unsuccessful because they failed to *read* the questions correctly.

7) Answer all questions

Unless you have been instructed that a penalty will be deducted for incorrect answers, it is better to guess than to omit a question.

8) Speed tests

It is often better NOT to guess on speed tests. It has been found that on timed tests people are tempted to spend the last few seconds before time is called in marking answers at random – without even reading them – in the hope of picking up a few extra points. To discourage this practice, the instructions may warn you that your score will be "corrected" for guessing. That is, a penalty will be applied. The incorrect answers will be deducted from the correct ones, or some other penalty formula will be used.

9) Review your answers

If you finish before time is called, go back to the questions you guessed or omitted to give them further thought. Review other answers if you have time.

10) Return your test materials

If you are ready to leave before others have finished or time is called, take ALL your materials to the monitor and leave quietly. Never take any test material with you. The monitor can discover whose papers are not complete, and taking a test booklet may be grounds for disqualification.

VIII. EXAMINATION TECHNIQUES

1) Read the general instructions carefully. These are usually printed on the first page of the exam booklet. As a rule, these instructions refer to the timing of the examination; the fact that you should not start work until the signal and must stop work at a signal, etc. If there are any *special* instructions, such as a choice of questions to be answered, make sure that you note this instruction carefully.

2) When you are ready to start work on the examination, that is as soon as the signal has been given, read the instructions to each question booklet, underline any key words or phrases, such as *least, best, outline, describe* and the like. In this way you will tend to answer as requested rather than discover on reviewing your paper that you *listed without describing*, that you selected the *worst* choice rather than the *best* choice, etc.

3) If the examination is of the objective or multiple-choice type – that is, each question will also give a series of possible answers: A, B, C or D, and you are called upon to select the best answer and write the letter next to that answer on your answer paper – it is advisable to start answering each question in turn. There may be anywhere from 50 to 100 such questions in the three or four hours allotted and you can see how much time would be taken if you read through all the questions before beginning to answer any. Furthermore, if you come across a question or group of questions which you know would be difficult to answer, it would undoubtedly affect your handling of all the other questions.

4) If the examination is of the essay type and contains but a few questions, it is a moot point as to whether you should read all the questions before starting to answer any one. Of course, if you are given a choice – say five out of seven and the like – then it is essential to read all the questions so you can eliminate the two that are most difficult. If, however, you are asked to answer all the questions, there may be danger in trying to answer the easiest one first because you may find that you will spend too much time on it. The best technique is to answer the first question, then proceed to the second, etc.

5) Time your answers. Before the exam begins, write down the time it started, then add the time allowed for the examination and write down the time it must be completed, then divide the time available somewhat as follows:
   - If 3-1/2 hours are allowed, that would be 210 minutes. If you have 80 objective-type questions, that would be an average of 2-1/2 minutes per question. Allow yourself no more than 2 minutes per question, or a total of 160 minutes, which will permit about 50 minutes to review.
   - If for the time allotment of 210 minutes there are 7 essay questions to answer, that would average about 30 minutes a question. Give yourself only 25 minutes per question so that you have about 35 minutes to review.

6) The most important instruction is to *read each question* and make sure you know what is wanted. The second most important instruction is to *time yourself properly* so that you answer every question. The third most important instruction is to *answer every question.* Guess if you have to but include something for each question. Remember that you will receive no credit for a blank and will probably receive some credit if you write something in answer to an essay question. If you guess a letter – say "B" for a multiple-choice question – you may have guessed right. If you leave a blank as an answer to a multiple-choice question, the examiners may respect your feelings but it will not add a point to your score. Some exams may penalize you for wrong answers, so in such cases *only*, you may not want to guess unless you have some basis for your answer.

7) Suggestions
   a. Objective-type questions
      1. Examine the question booklet for proper sequence of pages and questions
      2. Read all instructions carefully
      3. Skip any question which seems too difficult; return to it after all other questions have been answered
      4. Apportion your time properly; do not spend too much time on any single question or group of questions

5. Note and underline key words – *all, most, fewest, least, best, worst, same, opposite,* etc.
6. Pay particular attention to negatives
7. Note unusual option, e.g., unduly long, short, complex, different or similar in content to the body of the question
8. Observe the use of "hedging" words – *probably, may, most likely,* etc.
9. Make sure that your answer is put next to the same number as the question
10. Do not second-guess unless you have good reason to believe the second answer is definitely more correct
11. Cross out original answer if you decide another answer is more accurate; do not erase until you are ready to hand your paper in
12. Answer all questions; guess unless instructed otherwise
13. Leave time for review

b. Essay questions
   1. Read each question carefully
   2. Determine exactly what is wanted. Underline key words or phrases.
   3. Decide on outline or paragraph answer
   4. Include many different points and elements unless asked to develop any one or two points or elements
   5. Show impartiality by giving pros and cons unless directed to select one side only
   6. Make and write down any assumptions you find necessary to answer the questions
   7. Watch your English, grammar, punctuation and choice of words
   8. Time your answers; don't crowd material

8) Answering the essay question

Most essay questions can be answered by framing the specific response around several key words or ideas. Here are a few such key words or ideas:

M's: manpower, materials, methods, money, management
P's: purpose, program, policy, plan, procedure, practice, problems, pitfalls, personnel, public relations

a. Six basic steps in handling problems:
   1. Preliminary plan and background development
   2. Collect information, data and facts
   3. Analyze and interpret information, data and facts
   4. Analyze and develop solutions as well as make recommendations
   5. Prepare report and sell recommendations
   6. Install recommendations and follow up effectiveness

b. Pitfalls to avoid
   1. *Taking things for granted* – A statement of the situation does not necessarily imply that each of the elements is necessarily true; for example, a complaint may be invalid and biased so that all that can be taken for granted is that a complaint has been registered

2. *Considering only one side of a situation* – Wherever possible, indicate several alternatives and then point out the reasons you selected the best one
3. *Failing to indicate follow up* – Whenever your answer indicates action on your part, make certain that you will take proper follow-up action to see how successful your recommendations, procedures or actions turn out to be
4. *Taking too long in answering any single question* – Remember to time your answers properly

IX. AFTER THE TEST

Scoring procedures differ in detail among civil service jurisdictions although the general principles are the same. Whether the papers are hand-scored or graded by machine we have described, they are nearly always graded by number. That is, the person who marks the paper knows only the number – never the name – of the applicant. Not until all the papers have been graded will they be matched with names. If other tests, such as training and experience or oral interview ratings have been given, scores will be combined. Different parts of the examination usually have different weights. For example, the written test might count 60 percent of the final grade, and a rating of training and experience 40 percent. In many jurisdictions, veterans will have a certain number of points added to their grades.

After the final grade has been determined, the names are placed in grade order and an eligible list is established. There are various methods for resolving ties between those who get the same final grade – probably the most common is to place first the name of the person whose application was received first. Job offers are made from the eligible list in the order the names appear on it. You will be notified of your grade and your rank as soon as all these computations have been made. This will be done as rapidly as possible.

People who are found to meet the requirements in the announcement are called "eligibles." Their names are put on a list of eligible candidates. An eligible's chances of getting a job depend on how high he stands on this list and how fast agencies are filling jobs from the list.

When a job is to be filled from a list of eligibles, the agency asks for the names of people on the list of eligibles for that job. When the civil service commission receives this request, it sends to the agency the names of the three people highest on this list. Or, if the job to be filled has specialized requirements, the office sends the agency the names of the top three persons who meet these requirements from the general list.

The appointing officer makes a choice from among the three people whose names were sent to him. If the selected person accepts the appointment, the names of the others are put back on the list to be considered for future openings.

That is the rule in hiring from all kinds of eligible lists, whether they are for typist, carpenter, chemist, or something else. For every vacancy, the appointing officer has his choice of any one of the top three eligibles on the list. This explains why the person whose name is on top of the list sometimes does not get an appointment when some of the persons lower on the list do. If the appointing officer chooses the second or third eligible, the No. 1 eligible does not get a job at once, but stays on the list until he is appointed or the list is terminated.

X. HOW TO PASS THE INTERVIEW TEST

The examination for which you applied requires an oral interview test. You have already taken the written test and you are now being called for the interview test – the final part of the formal examination.

You may think that it is not possible to prepare for an interview test and that there are no procedures to follow during an interview. Our purpose is to point out some things you can do in advance that will help you and some good rules to follow and pitfalls to avoid while you are being interviewed.

What is an interview supposed to test?

The written examination is designed to test the technical knowledge and competence of the candidate; the oral is designed to evaluate intangible qualities, not readily measured otherwise, and to establish a list showing the relative fitness of each candidate – as measured against his competitors – for the position sought. Scoring is not on the basis of "right" and "wrong," but on a sliding scale of values ranging from "not passable" to "outstanding." As a matter of fact, it is possible to achieve a relatively low score without a single "incorrect" answer because of evident weakness in the qualities being measured.

Occasionally, an examination may consist entirely of an oral test – either an individual or a group oral. In such cases, information is sought concerning the technical knowledges and abilities of the candidate, since there has been no written examination for this purpose. More commonly, however, an oral test is used to supplement a written examination.

Who conducts interviews?

The composition of oral boards varies among different jurisdictions. In nearly all, a representative of the personnel department serves as chairman. One of the members of the board may be a representative of the department in which the candidate would work. In some cases, "outside experts" are used, and, frequently, a businessman or some other representative of the general public is asked to serve. Labor and management or other special groups may be represented. The aim is to secure the services of experts in the appropriate field.

However the board is composed, it is a good idea (and not at all improper or unethical) to ascertain in advance of the interview who the members are and what groups they represent. When you are introduced to them, you will have some idea of their backgrounds and interests, and at least you will not stutter and stammer over their names.

What should be done before the interview?

While knowledge about the board members is useful and takes some of the surprise element out of the interview, there is other preparation which is more substantive. It *is* possible to prepare for an oral interview – in several ways:

1) Keep a copy of your application and review it carefully before the interview

This may be the only document before the oral board, and the starting point of the interview. Know what education and experience you have listed there, and the sequence and dates of all of it. Sometimes the board will ask you to review the highlights of your experience for them; you should not have to hem and haw doing it.

2) Study the class specification and the examination announcement

Usually, the oral board has one or both of these to guide them. The qualities, characteristics or knowledges required by the position sought are stated in these documents. They offer valuable clues as to the nature of the oral interview. For example, if the job involves supervisory responsibilities, the announcement will usually indicate that knowledge of modern supervisory methods and the qualifications of the candidate as a supervisor will be tested. If so, you can expect such questions, frequently in the form of a hypothetical situation which you are expected to solve. NEVER go into an oral without knowledge of the duties and responsibilities of the job you seek.

3) Think through each qualification required

Try to visualize the kind of questions you would ask if you were a board member. How well could you answer them? Try especially to appraise your own knowledge and background in each area, *measured against the job sought*, and identify any areas in which you are weak. Be critical and realistic – do not flatter yourself.

4) Do some general reading in areas in which you feel you may be weak

For example, if the job involves supervision and your past experience has NOT, some general reading in supervisory methods and practices, particularly in the field of human relations, might be useful. Do NOT study agency procedures or detailed manuals. The oral board will be testing your understanding and capacity, not your memory.

5) Get a good night's sleep and watch your general health and mental attitude

You will want a clear head at the interview. Take care of a cold or any other minor ailment, and of course, no hangovers.

What should be done on the day of the interview?

Now comes the day of the interview itself. Give yourself plenty of time to get there. Plan to arrive somewhat ahead of the scheduled time, particularly if your appointment is in the fore part of the day. If a previous candidate fails to appear, the board might be ready for you a bit early. By early afternoon an oral board is almost invariably behind schedule if there are many candidates, and you may have to wait. Take along a book or magazine to read, or your application to review, but leave any extraneous material in the waiting room when you go in for your interview. In any event, relax and compose yourself.

The matter of dress is important. The board is forming impressions about you – from your experience, your manners, your attitude, and your appearance. Give your personal appearance careful attention. Dress your best, but not your flashiest. Choose conservative, appropriate clothing, and be sure it is immaculate. This is a business interview, and your appearance should indicate that you regard it as such. Besides, being well groomed and properly dressed will help boost your confidence.

Sooner or later, someone will call your name and escort you into the interview room. *This is it.* From here on you are on your own. It is too late for any more preparation. But remember, you asked for this opportunity to prove your fitness, and you are here because your request was granted.

What happens when you go in?

The usual sequence of events will be as follows: The clerk (who is often the board stenographer) will introduce you to the chairman of the oral board, who will introduce you to the other members of the board. Acknowledge the introductions before you sit down. Do not be surprised if you find a microphone facing you or a stenotypist sitting by. Oral interviews are usually recorded in the event of an appeal or other review.

Usually the chairman of the board will open the interview by reviewing the highlights of your education and work experience from your application – primarily for the benefit of the other members of the board, as well as to get the material into the record. Do not interrupt or comment unless there is an error or significant misinterpretation; if that is the case, do not hesitate. But do not quibble about insignificant matters. Also, he will usually ask you some question about your education, experience or your present job – partly to get you to start talking and to establish the interviewing "rapport." He may start the actual questioning, or turn it over to one of the other members. Frequently, each member undertakes the questioning on a particular area, one in which he is perhaps most competent, so you can expect each member to participate in the examination. Because time is limited, you may also expect some rather abrupt switches in the direction the questioning takes, so do not be upset by it. Normally, a board member will not pursue a single line of questioning unless he discovers a particular strength or weakness.

After each member has participated, the chairman will usually ask whether any member has any further questions, then will ask you if you have anything you wish to add. Unless you are expecting this question, it may floor you. Worse, it may start you off on an extended, extemporaneous speech. The board is not usually seeking more information. The question is principally to offer you a last opportunity to present further qualifications or to indicate that you have nothing to add. So, if you feel that a significant qualification or characteristic has been overlooked, it is proper to point it out in a sentence or so. Do not compliment the board on the thoroughness of their examination – they have been sketchy, and you know it. If you wish, merely say, "No thank you, I have nothing further to add." This is a point where you can "talk yourself out" of a good impression or fail to present an important bit of information. Remember, *you close the interview yourself.*

The chairman will then say, "That is all, Mr. ______, thank you." Do not be startled; the interview is over, and quicker than you think. Thank him, gather your belongings and take your leave. Save your sigh of relief for the other side of the door.

How to put your best foot forward

Throughout this entire process, you may feel that the board individually and collectively is trying to pierce your defenses, seek out your hidden weaknesses and embarrass and confuse you. Actually, this is not true. They are obliged to make an appraisal of your qualifications for the job you are seeking, and they want to see you in your best light. Remember, they must interview all candidates and a non-cooperative candidate may become a failure in spite of their best efforts to bring out his qualifications. Here are 15 suggestions that will help you:

1) Be natural – Keep your attitude confident, not cocky

If you are not confident that you can do the job, do not expect the board to be. Do not apologize for your weaknesses, try to bring out your strong points. The board is interested in a positive, not negative, presentation. Cockiness will antagonize any board member and make him wonder if you are covering up a weakness by a false show of strength.

2) Get comfortable, but don't lounge or sprawl

Sit erectly but not stiffly. A careless posture may lead the board to conclude that you are careless in other things, or at least that you are not impressed by the importance of the occasion. Either conclusion is natural, even if incorrect. Do not fuss with your clothing, a pencil or an ashtray. Your hands may occasionally be useful to emphasize a point; do not let them become a point of distraction.

3) Do not wisecrack or make small talk

This is a serious situation, and your attitude should show that you consider it as such. Further, the time of the board is limited – they do not want to waste it, and neither should you.

4) Do not exaggerate your experience or abilities

In the first place, from information in the application or other interviews and sources, the board may know more about you than you think. Secondly, you probably will not get away with it. An experienced board is rather adept at spotting such a situation, so do not take the chance.

5) If you know a board member, do not make a point of it, yet do not hide it

Certainly you are not fooling him, and probably not the other members of the board. Do not try to take advantage of your acquaintanceship – it will probably do you little good.

6) Do not dominate the interview

Let the board do that. They will give you the clues – do not assume that you have to do all the talking. Realize that the board has a number of questions to ask you, and do not try to take up all the interview time by showing off your extensive knowledge of the answer to the first one.

7) Be attentive

You only have 20 minutes or so, and you should keep your attention at its sharpest throughout. When a member is addressing a problem or question to you, give him your undivided attention. Address your reply principally to him, but do not exclude the other board members.

8) Do not interrupt

A board member may be stating a problem for you to analyze. He will ask you a question when the time comes. Let him state the problem, and wait for the question.

9) Make sure you understand the question

Do not try to answer until you are sure what the question is. If it is not clear, restate it in your own words or ask the board member to clarify it for you. However, do not haggle about minor elements.

10) Reply promptly but not hastily

A common entry on oral board rating sheets is "candidate responded readily," or "candidate hesitated in replies." Respond as promptly and quickly as you can, but do not jump to a hasty, ill-considered answer.

11) Do not be peremptory in your answers

A brief answer is proper – but do not fire your answer back. That is a losing game from your point of view. The board member can probably ask questions much faster than you can answer them.

12) Do not try to create the answer you think the board member wants

He is interested in what kind of mind you have and how it works – not in playing games. Furthermore, he can usually spot this practice and will actually grade you down on it.

13) Do not switch sides in your reply merely to agree with a board member

Frequently, a member will take a contrary position merely to draw you out and to see if you are willing and able to defend your point of view. Do not start a debate, yet do not surrender a good position. If a position is worth taking, it is worth defending.

14) Do not be afraid to admit an error in judgment if you are shown to be wrong

The board knows that you are forced to reply without any opportunity for careful consideration. Your answer may be demonstrably wrong. If so, admit it and get on with the interview.

15) Do not dwell at length on your present job

The opening question may relate to your present assignment. Answer the question but do not go into an extended discussion. You are being examined for a *new* job, not your present one. As a matter of fact, try to phrase ALL your answers in terms of the job for which you are being examined.

Basis of Rating

Probably you will forget most of these "do's" and "don'ts" when you walk into the oral interview room. Even remembering them all will not ensure you a passing grade. Perhaps you did not have the qualifications in the first place. But remembering them will help you to put your best foot forward, without treading on the toes of the board members.

Rumor and popular opinion to the contrary notwithstanding, an oral board wants you to make the best appearance possible. They know you are under pressure – but they also want to see how you respond to it as a guide to what your reaction would be under the pressures of the job you seek. They will be influenced by the degree of poise you display, the personal traits you show and the manner in which you respond.

ABOUT THIS BOOK

This book contains tests divided into Examination Sections. Go through each test, answering every question in the margin. We have also attached a sample answer sheet at the back of the book that can be removed and used. At the end of each test look at the answer key and check your answers. On the ones you got wrong, look at the right answer choice and learn. Do not fill in the answers first. Do not memorize the questions and answers, but understand the answer and principles involved. On your test, the questions will likely be different from the samples. Questions are changed and new ones added. If you understand these past questions you should have success with any changes that arise. Tests may consist of several types of questions. We have additional books on each subject should more study be advisable or necessary for you. Finally, the more you study, the better prepared you will be. This book is intended to be the last thing you study before you walk into the examination room. Prior study of relevant texts is also recommended. NLC publishes some of these in our Fundamental Series. Knowledge and good sense are important factors in passing your exam. Good luck also helps. So now study this Passbook, absorb the material contained within and take that knowledge into the examination. Then do your best to pass that exam.

EXAMINATION SECTION

EXAMINATION SECTION
TEST 1

DIRECTIONS: Each question or incomplete statement is followed by several suggested answers or completions. Select the one that BEST answers the question or completes the statement. *PRINT THE LETTER OF THE CORRECT ANSWER IN THE SPACE AT THE RIGHT.*

1. In performing a systems study, the analyst may find it necessary to prepare an accurate record of working statistics from departmental forms, questionnaires, and information gleaned in interviews.
   Which one of the following statements dealing with the statistical part of the study is the MOST valid?

   A. The emphasis of every survey is data collection.
   B. Data should not be represented in narrative form.
   C. The statistical report should include the titles of personnel required for each processing task.
   D. In gathering facts, the objective of a systems study should be the primary consideration

2. The most direct method of obtaining information about activities in the area under study is by observation. There are several general rules for an analyst that are essential for observing and being accepted as an observer.
   The one of the following statements relating to this aspect of an analyst's responsibility that is most valid in the initial phase is that the analyst should NOT

   A. limit himself to observing only; he may criticize operations and methods
   B. prepare himself for what he is about to observe
   C. obtain permission of the department's management to actually perform some of the clerical tasks himself
   D. offer views of impending charges regarding new staff requirements, equipment, or procedures

3. The active concern of the systems analyst is the study and documentation of what he observes as it exists. Before attempting the actual study and documentation, the analyst should comply with certain generally accepted procedures.
   Of the following, the step the analyst should *generally lake* FIRST is to

   A. define the problem and prepare a statement of objectives
   B. confer with the project director concerning persons to be interviewed
   C. accumulate data from all available sources within the area under study
   D. meet with operations managers to enlist their cooperation

4. During the course of any systems study, the analyst will have to gather some statistics if the operation model is to be realistic and meaningful.
   With respect to the statistical report part of the study, it is MOST valid to say that

A. it must follow a standard format since there should be no variation from one study to the next
B. the primary factor to be considered is the volume of work in the departmental unit at each stage of completion
C. only variations that occur during peak and slow periods should be recorded
D. unless deadlines in the departmental units studied by the analyst occur constantly, they should not be taken into account

5. In systems analysis, the interview is one of the analyst's major sources of information. In conducting an interview, he should strive for immediate rapport with the operations manager or department head with whom he deals.
With respect to his responsibility in this area, it is considered LEAST appropriate for the analyst to

A. explain the full background of the study and the scope of the investigation
B. emphasize the importance of achieving the stated objectives and review the plan of the project
C. assume that the attitudes of the workers are less important than those of the executives
D. request the manager's assistance in the form of questions, suggestions, and general cooperation

6. Large, complex endeavors often take a long time to implement. The following statements relate to long lead times imposed by large-scale endeavors.
Select the one usually considered to be LEAST valid.

A. Where there are external sponsors who provide funds or political support, they should be provided with some demonstration of what is being accomplished.
B. Long lead times simplify planning and diminish the threat of obsolescence by assuring that objectives will be updated by the time the project is nearing completion.
C. During the period when no tangible results are forthcoming, techniques must be found to assess progress.
D. Employees, particularly scientific personnel, should feel a sense of accomplishment or they may shy away from research which involves long-term commitments.

7. In traditional management theory, administrators are expected to collect and weigh facts and probabilities, make an optimal decision and see that it is carried out.
In the management of large-scale development projects, such a clear sequence of action is *generally* NOT possible because of

A. their limited duration
B. the static and fixed balance of power among interest groups
C. continuous suppression of new facts
D. constantly changing constraints and pressures

Questions 8-10.

DIRECTIONS: One of the most valuable parts of the systems package is the systems flowchart, a technique that aids understanding of the work flow. A flowchart should depict all the intricacies of the work flow from start to finish in order to give the onlooker a solid picture at a glance. The table below contains symbols used by the analyst in flowcharting. In answering Questions 8 through 10, refer to the following figures.

Figure I

Figure II

Figure III

Figure IV

Figure V

Figure VI

Figure VII

Figure VIII

Figure IX

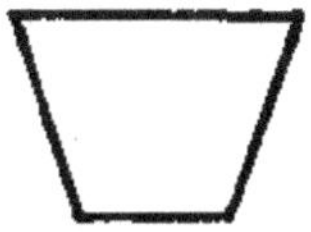
Figure X

Figure XI

Figure XII

Figure XIII

8. The symbol that is COMMONLY used to specify clerical procedures which are not essential to the main processing function and yet are part of the overall procedure is represented by Figure

   A. III B. VI C. XII D. XIII

9. An analyst wishes to designate the following activities:
   File reports; Calculate average; Attach labels.
   The MOST APPROPRIATE symbol to use is represented by Figure

   A. V B. VI C. VII D. II

10. A *Report, Journal,* or *Record* should be represented by Figure

   A. I B. III C. IX D. XI

Question 11.

DIRECTIONS: The following figures are often used in program and systems flowcharting.

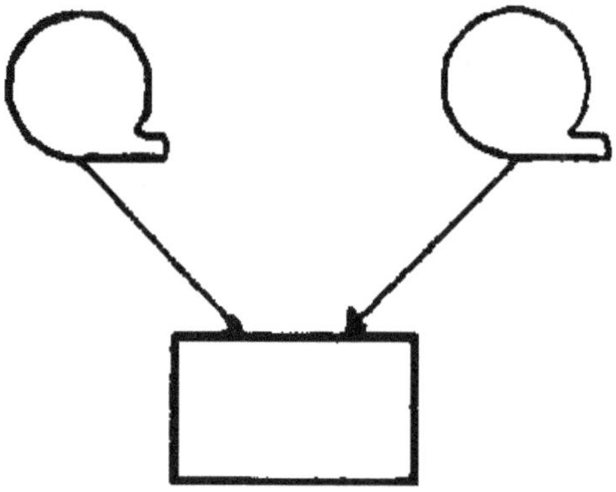

11. The above figures represent

    A. two storage discs incorporated in a processing function
    B. two report papers to be put in a cabinet in chronological order
    C. two transmittal tapes—both externally generated—routed to a vault
    D. an auxiliary operation involving two sequential decisions

12. When research and analysis of government programs, e.g., pest control, drug rehabilitation, etc., is sponsored and conducted within a government unit, the scope of the analysis should *generally* be ________ the scope of the authority of the manager to whom the analyst is responsible.

    A. less than
    B. less than or equal to
    C. greater than or equal to
    D. greater than

13. In recent years, there has been an increasing emphasis on outputs—the goods and services that a program produces. This emphasis on outputs imposes an information requirement. The one of the following which would MOST likely NOT be considered output information in a hospital or health care program is the

    A. number of patients cared for
    B. number of days patients were hospitalized
    C. budgeted monies for hospital beds
    D. quality of the service

14. Which one of the following statements pertaining to management information systems is generally considered to be LEAST valid?

    A. A management information system is a network of related subsystems developed according to an integrated scheme for evaluating the activities of an agency.
    B. A management information system specifies the content and format, the preparation and integration of information for all various functions within an agency that will best satisfy needs at various levels of management.
    C. To operate a successful management information system, an agency will require a complex electronic computer installation.
    D. The five elements which compose a management information system are: data input, files, data processing, procedures, and data output.

15. In the field of records management, electronic equipment is being used to handle office paperwork or data processing. With respect to such use, of the following, it is MOST valid to say that

    A. electronic equipment is not making great strides in the achievement of speed and economy in office paperwork
    B. electronic equipment accelerates the rate at which office paperwork is completed
    C. paperwork problems can be completely solved through mechanization
    D. introduction of electronic data processing equipment cuts down on the paper consumed in office processes

16. A reports control program evaluates the reporting requirements of top management so that reviews can be made of the existing reporting system to determine its adequacy. Of the following statements pertaining to reports control, which is the MOST likely to be characteristic of such a program?

    A. Only the exception will be reported
    B. Preparation of daily reports will be promoted
    C. Executives will not delegate responsibility for preparing reports
    D. Normal conditions are reported

17. Which of the following types of work measurement techniques requires the HIGHEST degree of training and skill of technicians and supervisors and is MOST likely to involve the HIGHEST original cost?

    A. Work sampling
    B. Predetermined time standards
    C. The time study (stopwatch timing)
    D. Employee reporting

18. Which of the following types of work measurement techniques *generally* requires the LEAST amount of time to measure and establish standards?

    A. Work sampling
    B. Predetermined time standards
    C. The time study (stopwatch timing)
    D. Employee reporting

19. Assume that you, as an analyst, have been assigned to formally organize small work groups within a city department to perform a special project. After studying the project, you find you must choose between two possible approaches—either task teams or highly functionalized groups.
    What would be one of the advantages of choosing the task-team approach over the highly functionalized organization?

    A. Detailed, centralized planning would be encouraged.
    B. Indifference to city goals and restrictions on output would be lessened.
    C. Work would be divided into very specialized areas.
    D. Superiors would be primarily concerned with seeing that subordinates do not deviate from the project.

20. In systems theory, there is a *what-if* method of treating uncertainty that explores the effect on the alternatives of environmental change. This method is generally referred to as ________ analysis.

A. sensitivity
B. contingency
C. a fortiori
D. systems

KEY (CORRECT ANSWERS)

1. D	11. A
2. D	12. B
3. A	13. C
4. B	14. C
5. C	15. B
6. B	16. A
7. D	17. B
8. D	18. A
9. A	19. B
10. B	20. B

TEST 2

DIRECTIONS: Each question or incomplete statement is followed by several suggested answers or completions. Select the one that BEST answers the question or completes the statement. *PRINT THE LETTER OF THE CORRECT ANSWER IN THE SPACE AT THE RIGHT.*

1. Which of the following systems exists at the strategic level of an organization?

   A. Decision support system (DSS)
   B. Executive support system (ESS)
   C. Knowledge work system (KWS)
   D. Management information system (MIS)

2. The functions of knowledge workers in an organization generally include each of the following EXCEPT

   A. updating knowledge
   B. managing documentation of knowledge
   C. serving as internal consultants
   D. acting as change agents

3. Which of the following is not a management benefit associated with end-user development of information systems?

   A. Reduced application backlog
   B. Increased user satisfaction
   C. Simplified testing and documentation procedures
   D. Improved requirements determination

4. Assume that an analyst is preparing an analysis of a departmental program. His investigation leads him to a potential problem relating to the program. The analyst thinks the potential problem is so serious that he cannot rely on preventive actions to remove the cause or significantly reduce the probability of its occurrence.
   Of the following, the MOST appropriate way for the analyst to promptly handle this serious matter described above would be to

   A. apply systematic afterthought to the achievement of objectives by analysis of the problem
   B. compare actual performance with the expected standard of performance
   C. prepare contingency actions to be adopted immediately if the problem does occur
   D. identify, locate, and describe the deviation from the standard

5. Assume that an analyst is directed to investigate a problem relating to organizational behavior in his agency and to prepare a report thereon. After reviewing the preliminary draft, his superior cautions him to overcome his tendency to misuse and overgeneralize his interpretation of existing knowledge.
   Which one of the following statements appearing in the draft is MOST *usually* considered to be a common distortion of behavioral science knowledge?

   A. Pay—even incentive pay—isn't very important anymore.
   B. There are nonrational aspects to people's behavior.
   C. The informal system exerts much control over organizational participants.
   D. Employees have many motives.

Questions 6-10.

DIRECTIONS: Each of Questions 6 through 10 consists of a statement which contains one word that is incorrectly used because it is not in keeping with the meaning that the quotation is evidently intended to convey. Determine which word is incorrectly used. Then select from the words lettered A, B, C, or D the word which, when substituted for the incorrectly used word, would BEST help to convey the meaning of the statement.

6. While the utilization of cost-benefit analysis in decision-making processes should be encouraged, it must be well understood that there are many limitations on the constraints of the analysis. One must be cautioned against using cost-benefit procedures automatically and blindly. Still, society will almost certainly be better off with the application of cost-benefit methods than it would be without them. As some authorities aptly point out, an important advantage of a cost-benefit study is that it forces those responsible to quantify costs and benefits as far as possible rather than rest content with vague qualitative judgments or personal hunches. Also, such an analysis has the very valuable byproduct of causing questions to be asked which would otherwise not have been raised. Finally, even if cost-benefit analysis cannot give the right answer, it can sometimes play the purely negative role of screening projects and rejecting those answers which are obviously less promising.

A. precise
B. externally
C. applicability
D. unresponsiveness

7. The programming method used by the government should attempt to assess the costs and benefits of individual projects, in comparison with private and other public alternatives. The program, then, consists of the most meritorious projects that the budget will design. Meritorious projects excluded from the budget provide arguments for increasing its size. There are difficulties inherent in the specific project approach. The attempt is to apply profit criteria in public projects analogous to those used in evaluating private projects. This involves comparison of monetary values of present and future costs and benefits. But, in many important cases, such as highways, parkways, and bridges, the product of the government's investment does not directly enter the market economy. Consequently, evaluation requires imputation of market values. For example, the returns on a bridge have been estimated by attempting to value the time saved by users. Such measurements necessarily contain a strong, element of artificiality.

A. annulled B. expedient C. accommodate D. marginally

8. Consider the problem of budgeting for activities designed to alleviate poverty and rooted unemployment. Are skill retraining efforts better or worse investments than public works? Are they better or worse than subsidies or other special incentives to attract new industry? Or, at an even more fundamental level, is a dollar invested in an attempt to rehabilitate a mature, technologically displaced, educationally handicapped, unemployed man a better commitment than a comparable dollar invested in supporting the educational and technical preparation of his son for employment in a different line of work? The questions may look unreasonable, even unanswerable. But the fact is that they are implicitly answered in any budget decision in the defined problem area. The only subordinate issue is whether the answer rests on intuition and guess, or on a budget system that presents relevant information so organized as to contribute to rational analysis, planning, and decision-making.

A. incomplete
B. relevant
C. significant
D. speculate

9. Choices among health programs, on the basis of cost-benefit analysis, raise another set of ethical problems. Measuring discounted lifetime earnings does not reveal the value of alleviating pain and suffering; some diseases have a high death rate, others are debilitating, others are merely uncomfortable. In general, choices among health and education programs that are predicated on discounted lifetime earnings will structure the choice against those who have low earnings, those whose earnings will materialize only at some future point in time, or those whose participation in the labor force is limited. It may be an appropriate economic policy to reduce expenditures in areas that maximize the future level of national income. But the maximization of social welfare may dictate attention to considerations, such as equality of opportunity, that transcend the limitations of values defined in such narrow terms.

   A. concentrate   B. divergent   C. enforcing   D. favorably

10. Without defined and time-phased objectives, it is difficult to be critical of administrative performance. To level a charge of waste or malperformance at the managers of a public program is, of course, one of the more popular pastimes of any administration's loyal opposition. But it is a rare experience to find such a charge documented by the kind of precise cost-effectiveness measures that are the common test of the quality of management performance in a well-run organization. Those who take a professional view of management responsibility are even more concerned about the acceptance of the kind of information that would enable a manager to assess the progress and quality of his own performance and, as appropriate, to initiate corrective action before outside criticism can even start.

   A. absence   B. rebut   C. withdraw   D. impeded

11. What is the relationship between the cost of inputs and the value of outputs when the results obtained from a program can be measured in money? ________ ratio.

   A. Value administrative-cost
   B. Break-even point
   C. Variable-direct
   D. Cost-benefit

12. Some writers in the field of public expenditure have noted a disturbing tendency inherent in cost-benefit analysis. Which one of the following statements MOST accurately expresses their concern over the use of cost-benefit analysis? It

   A. encourages the attachment of monetary values to intangibles
   B. has a built-in neglect of measurable outcomes while emphasizing the nonmeasurable
   C. consciously exaggerates social values and overstates political values
   D. encourages emphasis of those costs and benefits that cannot be measured rather than those that can

13. In private industry, budgetary control begins logically with an estimate of sales and the income therefrom.
   Of the following, the term used in government which is MOST analogous to that of sales in private industry is

   A. borrowed funds
   B. the amount appropriated
   C. general overhead
   D. surplus funds

14. When constructing graphs of causally related variables, how should the variables be placed to conform to conventional use?

    A. The independent variable should be placed on the vertical axis and the dependent variable on the horizontal axis.
    B. The dependent variable should be placed on the vertical axis and the independent variable on the horizontal axis.
    C. Independent variables should be placed on both axes.
    D. Dependent variables should be placed on both axes.

Questions 15-18.

DIRECTIONS: Answer Questions 15 through 18 on the basis of the following graph describing the output of computer operators.

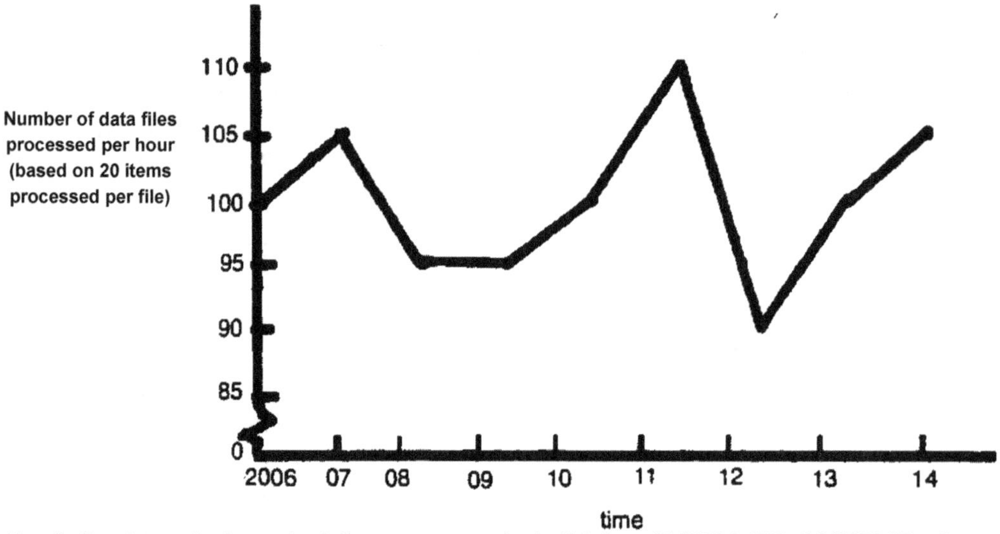

15. Of the following, during what four-year period did the AVERAGE OUTPUT of computer operators *fall below* 100 data files per hour?

    A. 2007-10   B. 2008-11   C. 2010-13   D. 2011-14

16. The AVERAGE PERCENTAGE CHANGE in output over the previous year's output for the years 2009 to 2012 is MOST NEARLY

    A. 2   B. 0   C. -5   D. -7

17. The DIFFERENCE between the actual output for 2012 and the projected figure based upon the average increase from 2006 to 2011 is MOST NEARLY

    A. 18   B. 20   C. 22   D. 24

18. Assume that after constructing the above graph, you, an analyst, discovered that the average number of items processed per file in 2012 was 25 (instead of 20) because of the complex nature of the work performed during that period.
The AVERAGE OUTPUT in files per hour for the period 2010 to 2013, expressed in terms of 20 items per file, would then be APPROXIMATELY

    A. 95   B. 100   C. 105   D. 110

19. Assume that Unit S's production fluctuated substantially from one year to another. In 2009, Unit S's production was 100% greater than in 2008; in 2010, it was 25% less than in 2009; and in 2011, it was 10% greater than in 2010. On the basis of this information, it is CORRECT to conclude that Unit S's production in 2011 exceeded its production in 2008 by

    A. 50%   B. 65%   C. 75%   D. 90%

20. Statistical sampling is often used in administrative operations primarily because it enables

    A. administrators to make staff selections
    B. decisions to be made based on mathematical and scientific fact
    C. courses of action to be determined by electronic data processing or computer programs
    D. useful predictions to be made from relatively small samples

---

KEY (CORRECT ANSWERS)

1.	B	11.	D
2.	B	12.	A
3.	C	13.	B
4.	C	14.	B
5.	A	15.	A
6.	C	16.	B
7.	C	17.	C
8.	C	18.	C
9.	A	19.	B
10.	A	20.	D

EXAMINATION SECTION
TEST 1

DIRECTIONS: Each question or incomplete statement is followed by several suggested answers or completions. Select the one that BEST answers the question or completes the statement. *PRINT THE LETTER OF THE CORRECT ANSWER IN THE SPACE AT THE RIGHT.*

1. Of the following factors, which one is LEAST important in determining the size of staff needed in conducting an organization survey?
The

   A. effectiveness of the personnel in supplying data for the study
   B. extent of report writing anticipated
   C. number of field locations and headquarters staff units to be covered
   D. number of individuals to be interviewed as part of fact finding

2. In planning a systems survey, which one of the following is MOST important in carrying out an effective survey after the purpose and scope of the survey has been determined? The

   A. format of the survey report
   B. methods and techniques to be employed
   C. personality problems which may materialize
   D. exact starting and completion dates

3. Which of the following is the BEST way of organizing a final report?

   A. Begin and end the report with a summary of conclusions showing how conclusions were changed as a result of findings and recommendations
   B. Begin the report with an overall summary and then place findings and recommendations in several sections
   C. Intertwine findings and conclusions in such a manner as to make the report readable and interesting
   D. Place the findings and recommendations in separate sections avoiding conclusions to the maximum extent possible

4. Which of the following disadvantages is the MOST serious in making reports verbally rather than in writing?

   A. An effective analyst may not be a good public speaker.
   B. Verbal reports are conveniently forgotten.
   C. It may not generate actions and follow-through by recipients.
   D. There is a lack of permanent record to which one may later refer.

5. Following a management survey, which of the following represents the MOST serious pitfall which may be made in recommending improvements?

   A. Failure to convince people of the benefits to be derived from the recommendations
   B. Failure to freely discuss recommendations with those who must live with them
   C. Tendency of the survey team to put their own personalities into the report
   D. Tendency to deal in personalities instead of dealing with objectives and sound management practices

6. A working outline for management analysts should include all of the following EXCEPT
   A. a chronological outline of the work steps
   B. a determination of background information needed
   C. the distribution of outline to key staff and line personnel
   D. preliminary conclusions

7. Which one of the following areas is the MOST critical for an analyst during the fact-finding stage of a study?
   A. Accuracy of data appearing in reports
   B. Attitude of those being interviewed by the analyst
   C. Observations and tentative conclusions reached by the analyst
   D. Suggestions and recommendations of interviewees

8. Creating an organization embraces all of the following areas of management EXCEPT
   A. clarification of objectives
   B. determining the number of people required to man the organization
   C. establishing operating budgets to make the plan effective
   D. proper structuring of all key positions

9. In an organization, the MAJOR barrier to accepting change is the
   A. assumption by management that everyone will willingly accept change
   B. failure by management to present proposed changes in a proper fashion
   C. lack of adaptive abilities on the part of employees
   D. lack of understanding on the part of employees of sound management principles

10. A supervisor who wishes to attain established objectives should concentrate on
    A. determining whether management is operating at maximum effectiveness
    B. making suggestions for improving the organization
    C. planning work assignments
    D. securing salary increases for needy employees

11. A usually competent employee complains that he does not understand the procedures to be followed in performing a certain task although the supervisor has explained them twice and has demonstrated them.
    Of the following, the BEST course of action for the supervisor to take is to
    A. ask the employee whether he has any problems which are bothering him
    B. assign someone else to the job
    C. explain the procedures again and demonstrate at the same time
    D. have the employee perform the job while he watches and gives additional instructions

12. GENERALLY, in order to be completely qualified as a supervisor, a person

    A. should be able to perform exceptionally well at least one of the jobs he supervises and have some knowledge of the others
    B. must have an intimate working knowledge of all facets of the jobs which he supervises
    C. should know the basic principles and procedures of the jobs he supervises
    D. need know little or nothing of the jobs which he supervises as long as he knows the principles of supervision

13. Which of the following contributes MOST to the problem of waste and inefficiency in offices?

    A. Cost control is a budget function primarily.
    B. Most organizations do not have soundly conceived budgets.
    C. Procedures improvement staffs have not as yet gained acceptance among white-collar workers.
    D. Supervisors generally are uninterested in making improvements.

14. Which of the following contributes MOST to the great number of duplicate reports and double-checking procedures frequently found in offices?
    The

    A. desire for protection
    B. desire to improve problem solving
    C. intent to *manage by exception*
    D. need for budget data

15. Which one of the following BEST identifies the narrow technician as compared with the broad-gauged analyst?
    He

    A. analyzes the activities of an agency
    B. attempts to form sound relationships with departmental personnel
    C. focuses attention on forms design and appearance
    D. follows work flow from one bureau to another by charting operational steps

16. The percentage of budget funds allocated to fixed overhead costs can be MOST effectively reduced by

    A. a soundly conceived *promotion from within* policy
    B. increasing the amount of work performed
    C. relocating to areas closer to the center of cities
    D. tightening the *fixed cost* portion of the budget

17. The term *span of control* USUALLY refers to

    A. individuals reporting to a common supervisor
    B. individuals with whom one individual has contact in the course of performing his assigned duties
    C. levels of supervision in an organization
    D. percentage of time in an organization devoted to supervisory duties

18. For an analyst, which of the following is generally LEAST important in conducting a management survey?

    A. Ability of employees to understand goals of the survey
    B. Attitude of supervisors of employees
    C. Availability of employees for interviews
    D. Cooperation of employees

19. Of the following, morale in an agency is generally MOST significantly affected by

    A. agency policies and procedures
    B. agency recognition of executives supporting agency goals
    C. the extent to which an agency meets its announced goals
    D. the number of management surveys conducted in an agency

20. Which of the following BEST describes the principle of *management by exception?*

    A. Allocating executive time and effort in direct relation to the dollar values of the budget
    B. Decentralizing management and dealing primarily with problem areas
    C. Measuring only direct costs
    D. Setting goals and objectives and managing only these

21. A WEAKNESS of many budgetary systems today is that they

    A. are subjectively determined by those most directly involved
    B. focus on management weakness rather than management strength
    C. only show variable costs
    D. show in detail why losses are occurring

22. Standards on which budgets are developed should be based PRIMARILY on

    A. a general consensus
    B. agency wishes
    C. analytical studies
    D. historical performance

23. The income, cost, and expense goals making up a budget are aimed at achieving a predetermined objective but do not necessarily measure the lowest possible costs. This is PRIMARILY so because

    A. budget committees are accounting-oriented and are not sympathetic with the supervisor's personnel problems
    B. budget committees fail to recognize the difference between direct and indirect costs
    C. the level of expenditures provided for in a budget by budget committees is frequently an arbitrary rather than a scientifically determined amount
    D. budget committees spend considerable time evaluating data to the point that the material gathered is not representative or current

24. Linear programming has all of the following characteristics EXCEPT: It

    A. is concerned with an optimum position in relation to some objective
    B. involves the selection among alternatives or the appropriate combination of alternatives
    C. not only requires that variables be qualitative but also rests on the assumption that the relations among the variables are minimized
    D. takes into account constraints or limits within which the decision is to be reached

25. In the PERT planning system, the time in which a non-critical task can slip schedule without holding up a project is USUALLY called

    A. constraint
    B. duration time
    C. dead time
    D. float or slack

26. The Produc-trol board and Schedugraphs are commercial variations of the ______ chart.

    A. flow
    B. Gantt
    C. layout
    D. multiple activity

27. The item which cannot be analyzed by such schematic techniques as the frequency polygon and the histogram is the

    A. age of accounts receivable
    B. morale and cohesiveness of work groups
    C. number of accidents in a plant
    D. wage pattern

28. An essential employee benefit of work measurement which FREQUENTLY is the key to the successful implementation of such a program is

    A. equitable work distribution
    B. facilitation of the development of budgets
    C. measurement and control of office productivity
    D. prevention of unfair work distribution

29. An organizational arrangement whereby different employees perform different work steps upon the same work items at the same time is called the ______ method.

    A. functional
    B. homogenous
    C. parallel or linear arrangement
    D. unit assembly

30. Frequently, opposition to a management survey stems from an executive's feeling that he might be considered responsible for the unsatisfactory conditions that the project is aimed at correcting.
    To overcome this type of opposition, the analyst should GENERALLY

    A. avoid the issue altogether
    B. face the situation *head on* and, if the executive is responsible, tell him so
    C. offer a reasonable explanation for those conditions early enough in the discussion to forestall any implication of criticism
    D. place the blame for the unsatisfactory conditions at the lowest level in the organization to avoid incriminating the boss

31. Which of the following situations is LEAST likely to require a management survey?

A. Changes in policy
B. Management requests for additional manpower
C. Legislation mandating changes in operating procedures
D. Significantly lower costs than anticipated

32. The efficiency of a procedure is often influenced by the practices or performance of departments that play no direct part in carrying it out.
In view of this, the analyst must

A. disregard the practices or performance of departments that play no direct part in the procedure
B. do the very best job within the department studied to compensate for the outside problems
C. ask for assistance in solving the problems created by this situation
D. study and evaluate the external factors to the extent that they bear on the problem

33. Which one of the following is NOT a key step in staff delegation and development?

A. Evaluation of the completed job
B. Preparation of a subordinate to accept additional duties
C. Review of daily progress
D. Selection of a suitable job to be delegated

34. Which one of the following is NOT an essential characteristic of effective delegation?

A. In delegating, the supervisor is no longer responsible.
B. The individual to whom authority is delegated must be accountable for fulfillment of the task.
C. The individual to whom authority is delegated must clearly understand this authority
D. The individual to whom authority is delegated must get honest recognition for a job well done.

35. Whenever a manager must determine how long an operation should take, he is involved with the problem of setting a time standard.
To PROPERLY set time standards, the manager must distinguish between

A. estimation processes and evaluation processes
B. performance of the slowest employee and performance of the fastest employee
C. stop watch study and work sampling
D. synthetic and arbitrary systems

36. Assuming a report is needed, which approach USUALLY facilitates implementation?
A

A. draft report submitted to key people for review, discussion, modification, and then resubmission in final form
B. report in final form which sets forth alternate recommended solutions
C. report which sets forth the problems and the recommended solution in conformance with the desires of those most directly involved
D. visual presentation with minimal report writing

37. Of the following elements, which is the LEAST important in writing a survey report?
A
    A. definite course of action to be followed
    B. listing of benefits to be gained through implementation
    C. review of opinions as differentiated from facts
    D. summary of conclusions

38. Physical appearance and accuracy are important features in gaining acceptance to recommendations. Which one of the following might be OVERLOOKED in preparing a report which is to have wide distribution?
    A. A comprehensive index
    B. An attractive binder
    C. Proper spacing and page layout
    D. Charts and tables

39. The elimination of meaningless reports, although reducing the total information output, IMPROVES the management process by
    A. determining the number of employees required to perform the work assigned
    B. identifying the difference between direct and indirect costs
    C. increasing the effectiveness of executives
    D. limiting the budget to variable costs

40. In determining whether or not to use a computerized system as opposed to a manual system, which of the following would normally have the MOST influence on the decision?
The
    A. availability of analysts and programmers to design and install the system
    B. availability of computer time
    C. basic premise that all computerized systems are superior to manual systems
    D. volume and complexity of transactions required

KEY (CORRECT ANSWERS)

1. A	11. D	21. A	31. D
2. B	12. C	22. C	32. D
3. B	13. C	23. C	33. C
4. D	14. A	24. C	34. A
5. D	15. C	25. D	35. A
6. D	16. B	26. B	36. A
7. C	17. A	27. B	37. C
8. C	18. A	28. A	38. B
9. B	19. A	29. D	39. C
10. C	20. B	30. C	40. D

TEST 2

DIRECTIONS: Each question or incomplete statement is followed by several suggested answers or completions. Select the one that BEST answers the question or completes the statement. *PRINT THE LETTER OF THE CORRECT ANSWER IN THE SPACE AT THE RIGHT*

1. The one of the following that is NOT normally involved in the development of a management information system is

   A. determination of the best method of preparing and presenting the required information
   B. determination of line and staff relationships within the various units of the organizational structure
   C. determination of what specific information is needed for decision-making and control
   D. identification of the critical aspects of the business, i.e., the end results and other elements of performance which need to be planned and controlled

2. The long-term growth in size and complexity of both business and government has increased management's dependence on more formal written summaries of operating results in place of the informal, on-the-spot observations and judgments of smaller organizations.
   In addition, there is a growing management need to

   A. increase the complexity of those phases of the management process which have previously been simplified
   B. increase the speed and accuracy of artificial intelligence
   C. measure the effectiveness of managerial performance
   D. reduce alcoholism by greatly limiting personal contacts between the various levels of management within the organization

3. Of the following, it is MOST essential that a management information system provide information needed for

   A. determining computer time requirements
   B. developing new office layouts
   C. drawing new organization charts
   D. planning and measuring results

4. The PRIMARY purpose of control reports is to

   A. compare actual performance with planned results
   B. determine staffing requirements
   C. determine the work flow
   D. develop a new budget

5. Which one of the following has the GREATEST negative impact on communications in a large organization?

   A. Delays in formulating variable policies relating to communications
   B. Failure to conduct comprehensive courses in communications skills
   C. Failure to get information to those who need it
   D. Unclear organizational objectives

6. Efficiency of an organization is significantly impacted by all of the following EXCEPT

   A. network connectivity
   B. software compatibility
   C. hardware upgrades
   D. cloud data storage

7. The type of computer configuration in which the data are processed at one time after they have been made a matter of record is known as

   A. batching
   B. in line
   C. off line
   D. real time

8. A computer configuration system in which the input or output equipment is directly connected and operates under control of the computer is known as

   A. off line
   B. on line
   C. random access
   D. real time

9. A manager who wants to quickly analyze the output of a particular department would most likely refer to which one of the following?

   A. An Excel spreadsheet with production data logged by department
   B. Email reports submitted by department leaders
   C. Quarterly reports describing production targets and measurements
   D. An Excel spreadsheet with employee-generated survey data related to typical daily output and capabilities

10. Computers are generally considered to consist of four major sections. The one of the following which is NOT a major section is

   A. buffer
   B. control
   C. processing
   D. storage

11. Of the following, administrative control is PRIMARILY dependent upon

   A. adequate information
   B. a widespread spy network
   C. strict supervisors
   D. strong sanctions

12. Meticulous care must be exercised in writing the methodology section of the research report so that

   A. another investigator will achieve the same results if he repeats the study
   B. the interpretation of the findings cannot be challenged
   C. the report will be well balanced
   D. the rules of scientific logic are clearly indicated

13. When data are grouped into a frequency distribution, the *true mode* by definition is the _____ in the distribution.

   A. 50% point
   B. largest single range
   C. point of greatest concentration
   D. smallest single range

14. Which of the following is LEAST likely to be a potential benefit arising from the use of electronic data processing systems?
    A. Analysis of more data and analysis of data in greater depth than manual systems
    B. Increased speed and accuracy in information processing
    C. Lower capital expenditures for office equipment
    D. Reduced personnel costs in tabulating and reporting functions

15. A *grapevine* is BEST defined as
    A. a harmful method of communication
    B. a system of communication operative below the executive level
    C. an informal communication system of no functional importance to an organization
    D. the internal and non-systematic channel of communication within an organization

16. Of the following, the symbol shown at the right, as used in a systems flow chart, means

    A. document
    B. manual operation
    C. planning
    D. process

17. The mean age of a sample group drawn from population X is 37.5 years and the standard error of the mean is 5.9. There is a *99%* probability that the computed mean age of other samples drawn from population X would fall within the range of
    A. 31.6–43.4
    B. 26.0–52.7
    C. 22.2–52.8
    D. 20.0–55.0

18. After a budget has been developed, it serves to
    A. assist the accounting department in posting expenditures
    B. measure the effectiveness of department managers
    C. provide a yardstick against which actual costs are measured
    D. provide the operating department with total expenditures to date

19. In order to ensure that work measurement or time study results will be consistent from one study to another, and reflect a fair day's work, the performance of the clerks must be rated or levelled.
Which of the following is LEAST likely to be included among the techniques for determining the performance level or for rating the study?
    A. Predetermined times
    B. Published rating tables
    C. Sampling studies
    D. Training films

20. Of the following, the BEST practice to follow when training a new employee is to
    A. encourage him to feel free to ask questions at any time
    B. immediately demonstrate how fast his job can be done so he will know what is expected of him
    C. let him watch other employees for a week or two
    D. point out mistakes after completion so he will learn by experience

21. An IMPORTANT aspect to keep in mind during the decision-making process is that

    A. all possible alternatives for attaining goals should be sought out and considered
    B. considering various alternatives only leads to confusion
    C. once a decision has been made, it cannot be retracted
    D. there is only one correct method to reach any goal

22. Implementation of accountability REQUIRES

    A. a leader who will not hesitate to take punitive action
    B. an established system of communication from the bottom to the top
    C. explicit directives from leaders
    D. too much expense to justify it

23. Of the following, the MAJOR difference between systems and procedures analysis and work simplification is:

    A. The former complicates organizational routine and the latter simplifies it
    B. The former is objective and the latter is subjective
    C. The former generally utilizes expert advice and the latter is a *do-it-yourself* improvement by supervisors and workers
    D. There is no difference other than in name

24. Systems development is concerned with providing

    A. a specific set of work procedures
    B. an overall framework to describe general relationships
    C. definitions of particular organizational functions
    D. organizational symbolism

25. Organizational systems and procedures should be

    A. developed as problems arise as no design can anticipate adequately the requirements of an organization
    B. developed jointly by experts in systems and procedures and the people who are responsible for implementing them
    C. developed solely by experts in systems and procedures
    D. eliminated whenever possible to save unnecessary expense

26. The CHIEF danger of a decentralized control system is that

    A. excessive reports and communications will be generated
    B. problem areas may not be detected readily
    C. the expense will become prohibitive
    D. this will result in too many *chiefs*

27. Of the following, management guides and controls clerical work PRINCIPALLY through

    A. close supervision and constant checking of personnel
    B. spot checking of clerical procedures
    C. strong sanctions for clerical supervisors
    D. the use of printed forms

28. Which of the following is MOST important before conducting fact-finding interviews?

    A. Becoming acquainted with all personnel to be interviewed
    B. Explaining the techniques you plan to use
    C. Explaining to the operating officials the purpose and scope of the study
    D. Orientation of the physical layout

29. Of the following, the one that is NOT essential in carrying out a comprehensive work improvement program is

    A. standards of performance
    B. supervisory training
    C. work count/task list
    D. work distribution chart

30. Which of the following control techniques is MOST useful on large, complex systems projects?

    A. A general work plan
    B. Gantt chart
    C. Monthly progress report
    D. PERT chart

31. The action which is MOST effective in gaining acceptance of a study by the agency which is being studied is

    A. a directive from the agency head to install a study based on recommendations included in a report
    B. a lecture-type presentation following approval of the procedures
    C. a written procedure in narrative form covering the proposed system with visual presentations and discussions
    D. procedural charts showing the *before* situation, forms, steps, etc. to the employees affected

32. Which of the following is NOT an advantage in the use of oral instructions as compared with written instructions? Oral instruction(s)

    A. can easily be changed
    B. is superior in transmitting complex directives
    C. facilitate exchange of information between a superior and his subordinate
    D. with discussions make it easier to ascertain understanding

33. Which organization principle is MOST closely related to procedural analysis and improvement?

    A. Duplication, overlapping, and conflict should be eliminated.
    B. Managerial authority should be clearly defined.
    C. The objectives of the organization should be clearly defined.
    D. Top management should be freed of burdensome detail.

34. Which one of the following is the MAJOR objective of operational audits?

    A. Detecting fraud
    B. Determining organization problems
    C. Determining the number of personnel needed
    D. Recommending opportunities for improving operating and management practices

35. Of the following, the formalization of organization structure is BEST achieved by

   A. a narrative description of the plan of organization
   B. functional charts
   C. job descriptions together with organization charts
   D. multi-flow charts

36. Budget planning is MOST useful when it achieves

   A. cost control
   B. forecast of receipts
   C. performance review
   D. personnel reduction

37. The UNDERLYING principle of sound administration is to

   A. base administration on investigation of facts
   B. have plenty of resources available
   C. hire a strong administrator
   D. establish a broad policy

38. Although questionnaires are not the best survey tool the management analyst has to use, there are times when a good questionnaire can expedite the *fact-finding* phase of a management survey.
Which of the following should be AVOIDED in the design and distribution of the questionnaire?

   A. Questions should be framed so that answers can be classified and tabulated for analysis.
   B. Those receiving the questionnaire must be knowledgeable enough to accurately provide the information desired.
   C. The questionnaire should enable the respondent to answer in a narrative manner.
   D. The questionnaire should require a minimum amount of writing.

39. Of the following, the formula which is used to calculate the arithmetic mean from data grouped in a frequency distribution is:
M =

   A. $\frac{n}{\Sigma fx}$
   B. $N(\Sigma fx)$
   C. $\frac{\Sigma fx}{N}$
   D. $\frac{\Sigma x}{fN}$

40. Arranging large groups of numbers in frequency distributions

   A. gives a more composite picture of the total group than a random listing
   B. is misleading in most cases
   C. is unnecessary in most instances
   D. presents the data in a form whereby further manipulation of the group is eliminated

KEY (CORRECT ANSWERS)

1. B	11. A	21. A	31. C
2. C	12. A	22. B	32. B
3. D	13. C	23. C	33. A
4. A	14. C	24. B	34. D
5. C	15. D	25. B	35. C
6. C	16. B	26. B	36. A
7. A	17. C	27. D	37. A
8. B	18. C	28. C	38. C
9. A	19. C	29. B	39. C
10. A	20. A	30. D	40. A

EXAMINATION SECTION

TEST 1

DIRECTIONS: Each question or incomplete statement is followed by several suggested answers or completions. Select the one that BEST answers the question or completes the statement. *PRINT THE LETTER OF THE CORRECT ANSWER IN THE SPACE AT THE RIGHT.*

1. If an analyst recommends to the head of a newly established agency that the latter institute a line type of organization, he should also point out that this structure has the following MAJOR disadvantage: 1.____
   A. Delay will be encountered in reaching decisions.
   B. Coordination will be difficult to secure.
   C. Authority and responsibility will be diffused.
   D. Discipline will be hard to maintain.

2. Of the following statements which relate to the use of office space, the one that is LEAST valid is: 2.____
   A. A request for a conference room on the basis of privacy for meetings usually cannot be justified, for most private offices are suitable for meetings.
   B. Private offices are objectionable because they tend to slow up the work by interfering with supervisory effectiveness.
   C. The reception room should not handle ordinary and necessary traffic between different areas in the office.
   D. The space utilization of private offices is about 35 to 50 percent of that of the open area arrangement.

3. In preparing the layout for a small office, PARAMOUNT consideration should be given to a design that will 3.____
   A. accommodate the flows representing the largest volumes of work
   B. cause work to progress through its production cycle regardless of backtracking in a straight line or U
   C. increase the speed and movement of papers involved in the flow of work to the shortest compass feasible
   D. take into account vertical relationships of floor locations in the work flow

4. When centralization of office activities is instituted, which one of the following conditions will MOST likely occur? 4.____
   A. Confidentiality of office work will decrease.
   B. Equitable wage schedules will be undermined.
   C. Office machine maintenance costs will increase.
   D. Training of office employees will be delayed.

5. Descriptor is a term COMMONLY used in 5.____
   A. information retrieval
   B. network analysis
   C. planning and forecasting
   D. systems analysis

6. Of the following, the BEST way to secure effective management is USUALLY to 6.____
   A. allow staff agencies to help solve the administrative problems of line management
   B. provide a good organization structure
   C. select capable managers and administrators
   D. set up conservative spans of control

7. The MOST effective way of graphically representing the division of total costs into component costs as they vary over a period of time is by means of a 7.____
   A. band chart
   B. pictograph
   C. pie diagram
   D. histogram

8. During the past 50 years, the rate of increase in the number of office workers has been much greater than that of our total working force. 8.____
   The LEAST likely reason to cause this increase is the
   A. dispersal of clerical operations which accompanied the growth in manufacturing
   B. development of "service industries"
   C. use of more factual information by managers
   D. expansion in business legislation and governmental regulatory agencies

9. In attempting to discover flaws in an organization, an organization chart has been prepared. 9.____
   The condition that will be LEAST likely to be disclosed through use of the organization chart will be
   A. executives who are burdened with details
   B. work schedules that are unmet
   C. promotional possibilities that are not being provided
   D. functions which are becoming secondary due to splitting among departmental units

10. The PRIMARY function of systems analysis in the Planning Programming Budgetary System is to 10.____
   A. cost out various alternatives
   B. develop a PERT chart for evaluating program content
   C. develop better alternatives than those which are in the currently approved program
   D. provide perspective in judging the validity of an expenditure

11. Systems analysis would be LEAST effective in solving which of these problems? The 11.____
   A. determination of need for a new pier
   B. problem of air pollution
   C. selection of a site for a police station
   D. selection of engineering personnel

12. In procedural analysis, when the purpose of a particular step has been shown to be justifiable to the end purpose of the procedure, the NEXT necessary step is usually to 12.____
   A. determine the time limits for the step
   B. weigh the value of the step against the expense involved
   C. sell the idea to the supervisory staff
   D. make it a part of the procedure

13. ▽ is a symbol used in records management flow diagrams to indicate 13.____
   A. destruction of paper
   B. filing and/or permanent storage
   C. inspection
   D. microfilming is necessary

14. The concept that decisions should be made at the lowest level in an organization where all the (required) information and competence are available is MOST particularly a general rule in 14.____
   A. communications theory
   B. decentralization of authority
   C. incremental decision-making
   D. span of control

15. An office quality control program may comprise several approaches. The one LEAST desirable of the following normally is to 15.____
   A. follow a policy of spot or sample checking
   B. follow a practice of 100% checking of all work to verify its correctness
   C. inspect the work by means of a statistical quality control program
   D. review and tally errors being detected from present checking operations to determine the amount of checking presently being followed and the results being obtained

16. When a form is to be completed by an electronic data processing machine, which of the following is LEAST necessary? 16.____
   A. Form number
   B. Form title
   C. Lines
   D. Margins

17. Under a PPBS system, the selection of the proper alternative program should be made by the 17.____
   A. administrator responsible for the program, with the approval of the mayor and city legislative body
   B. budget director, basing his decision according to the optimum alternative
   C. budget examiner who reviews the administration budget
   D. chief systems analyst who programmed the alternatives

18. Which of the following is LEAST applicable in describing PPBS as a general concept? A 18.____
   A. quantitative method of budgeting for the coming year
   B. system of defining long-range alternative programs and planning the allocation of resources on the basis of the cost of the long-range program versus the benefit derived over the planning period
   C. system of measuring budgeted performance against pre-established goals
   D. system that establishes the importance of a program in terms of the expected cost of executing

19. Under a PPBS system, substantive planning is NORMALLY defined as 19.____
   A. fiscal planning
   B. planning of future budgets
   C. planning of objectives—ultimate and intermediate
   D. planning of programs—ultimate and intermediate

20. The method of selection which would provide the TIGHTEST standard under the logging method of work measurement would be 20.____
   A. one-third array
   B. modal average
   C. selected arithmetic average
   D. upper quartile

21. A concept for the evaluation of managers whereby goals are set and agreed upon for each manager, and then his attainment of those goals is evaluated at a particular prearranged target date, is BEST termed 21.____
   A. management by objectives
   B. management evaluation planning
   C. managerial performance appraisal
   D. program evaluation

22. When work is organized so that the work is broken into a series of jobs, and each unit of work (a customer order, invoice, etc.) moves progressively to position until completion, we would NORMALLY refer to this as the 22.____
   A. parallel plan of work subdivision
   B. serial plan
   C. unit assembly plan
   D. unit process plan

23. The type of organization in which employees report to a nominal manager for administrative purposes but are assigned to *ad hoc* supervisors as various assignments arise is BEST termed the _____ type of organization. 23.____
   A. functional
   B. process
   C. project or task force
   D. unit assembly

24. The expression which BEST defines a generalized situation in which several programs may be executed simultaneously or concurrently is 24.____
   A. multiprocessing
   B. multiprogramming
   C. on-line, real time programming
   D. process overlap

25. The sampling technique which consists of taking selections at constant intervals (every nth unit) from a list of the universe is called _____ sampling. 25.____
   A. area
   B. quota
   C. stratified random
   D. systematic

26. A method of project scheduling and control which shows the MOST optimistic, MOST pessimistic, and MOST probable estimate of time for how long each task in a project will take is called 26.____
   A. CPM (Critical Path Method)
   B. Gantt charting
   C. Linear Responsibility Charting
   D. PERT

27. The idea that classic organizational structure tends to create work situations having requirements counter to those for psychological success and self-esteem, sometimes called the "organizational dilemma," is MOST closely associated with which one of the following persons? 27.____
   A. Chris Argyris
   B. Frederick Taylor
   C. Luther Gulick
   D. Max Weber

28. Charles J. Hitch is known PRIMARILY for his work in the area of 28.____
   A. administrative behavior
   B. behavioral sciences
   C. organizational analysis
   D. PPBS

Questions 29-30.

DIRECTIONS: Questions 29 and 30 are to be answered on the basis of the following paragraph.

If one were to observe the information, in all its variant forms, that flows to a manager in the typical American enterprise, he would have a word for it: chaos. Subordinates want to be helpful, or to promote themselves, or to reflect discredit somewhere, and they originate or serve as a transmission belt for information they think the manager should have. Furthermore, it is the nature of the business process that information is generated where it is most easily reflected and is very scarce in areas or phases where data are not readily available. If one could project a tape which showed information density through time, he would find areas of heavy concentration and areas of little or no cloudiness. This means two things: First, people seem to have an inner drive to report available information in many ways, many forms, and for many users. Note what an accountant or statistician can do with two figures—or a mathematician without any figures at all! Second, the lack of information in specific areas means only that it is not available; it does not mean that it is unnecessary. Indeed, the blind areas may be of the greatest importance for decision-making purposes.

29. The result of the state of affairs described in the above paragraph would MOST likely be 29.____
   A. inconsequential
   B. an impetus to proper decision-making
   C. high costs and poor decisions
   D. a successful uniform information system

30. The author in this paragraph is PRIMARILY concerned with 30.____
   A. decision-making theory
   B. communications
   C. tape information systems
   D. information gathering by accountants and statisticians

KEY (CORRECT ANSWERS)

1.	B	11.	D	21.	A
2.	A	12.	B	22.	B
3.	A	13.	B	23.	C
4.	A	14.	B	24.	B
5.	A	15.	B	25.	D
6.	C	16.	C	26.	D
7.	A	17.	A	27.	A
8.	A	18.	A	28.	D
9.	B	19.	C	29.	C
10.	C	20.	D	30.	B

TEST 2

DIRECTIONS: Each question or incomplete statement is followed by several suggested answers or completions. Select the one that BEST answers the question or completes the statement. *PRINT THE LETTER OF THE CORRECT ANSWER IN THE SPACE AT THE RIGHT.*

1. It has been decided to make a few important revisions in the methods and procedures of a particular work unit. 1.____
   Of the following, the method of implementing these revisions which would probably be MOST desirable in terms of morale as well as efficiency is to
   A. give all the employees in the work unit individual instructions in the revised procedures, making sure that each employee fully understands the changes before instructing the next employee
   B. institute all the revisions at once, followed by on-the-job training for all the employees in the work unit
   C. introduce the revisions one at a time, accompanying each revision with an orientation for the employees
   D. set up a training course for the employees, instructing them in all aspects of the revised procedures prior to their implementation

2. In an administrative survey of a multiple-unit organization, which of the following is it usually MOST important to identify? The 2.____
   A. data and information used commonly by units, how used and by whom
   B. flow of data and information within a single organization unit
   C. type and volume of data used within individual units and transmitted between units
   D. way data and information are transmitted between units, how used and by whom

3. A noted authority has described a common method of making organizational policy in which the decision-maker tries to find some acceptable level of goal accomplishment short of ultimate fulfillment of all objectives and to frame policies toward such fulfillment. 3.____
   Of the following, this method is BEST termed
   A. feedback
   B. incrementalism
   C. satisfying
   D. seriality

4. The managerial grid, as defined by Blake and Mouton, shows two concerns and a range of interaction between them as follows: The horizontal axis indicates a concern for _____, while the vertical axis indicates a concern for _____. 4.____
   A. hierarchy; people
   B. production; people
   C. organization; people
   D. people; P/L (profit or loss)

5. In the managerial grid, which managerial style is dominant for any given person in any particular situation can be determined by any one or several sets of conditions in combination. 5.____
The five conditions in CORRECT order are:
   A. Organization, management, values, chance, production
   B. Organization, situation, values, personality, chance
   C. Production, situation, personality, chance, individually
   D. Values, personality, variety, organization, chance

6. The analyst may be faced with a choice of either recommending service contracts or recommending on-call service for maintenance of equipment. 6.____
In making a decision, the one of the following factors which would mitigate MOST against the use of on-call service would be that
   A. equipment utilization is not heavy
   B. prompt service when breakdowns occur is seldom essential
   C. regular checkups and servicing are considered desirable based on past equipment history
   D. trade-ins are made frequently

7. The type of paper stock MOST commonly used for office forms work is _____ bond. 7.____
   A. cotton content
   B. duplicating or mimeo
   C. rag
   C. sulphite

8. In laying out an office, according to most authorities, the amount of space which NORMALLY should be allowed for a clerk would in the range of _____ square feet. 8.____
   A. 10 to15
   B. 25 to 100
   C. 110 to 125
   D. 130 to 150

9. A noted behavioral scientist believes that the MOST important element in job satisfaction, of those listed below, s 9.____
   A. job security
   B. responsibility or recognition
   C. salary
   D. type of supervision

10. The point of view that the average human being prefers to be directed, wishes to avoid responsibility, has relatively little ambition, and wants security above all has been described in Douglas MacGregor's classic book on human motivation in business. 10.____
He includes this point of view in what he calls
   A. Theory X
   B. Theory Y
   C. Theory Z
   D. Theory X and Y combined

11. New desk top electronic machines are of two main types—printing or display. Display type machines show the results by any of the following methods EXCEPT for 11.____
   A. cathode ray tube
   B. electro-mechanical
   C. mosaic or liquid crystal
   D. nixie

12. The type of chart that is normally MOST useful for studying the work assignments and job content of individual positions in a particular organizational unit when making a procedure analysis is the _____ chart. 12._____
    A. columnar flow
    B. procedure flow
    C. work distribution
    D. work process

13. To prepare a work distribution chart, two other types of lists generally must be prepared. 13._____
    In the usual order of preparation, they are FIRST a(n)
    A. flow diagram, then an activity list
    B. skills list, then a task list
    C. task list, then an activity list
    D. activity list, then a task list

14. The critical path is defined as that path (or those paths) through a network 14,_____
    A. showing the least number of time units
    B. showing the greatest number of time units
    C. which consists (or consist) entirely of sequential activities
    D. which links (or link) together activities in concurrent relationship to each other

15. A statistical quality control program in the office is valuable in alerting management that the level of quality for particular transactions has deteriorated. 15._____
    It is, however, LEAST likely to reveal
    A. when preventive action is necessary
    B. when a variation is due to other than chance
    C. when an assignable cause is present
    D. what the cause of the error is

16. In work measurement, the value of a TMU is _____ min. 16._____
    A. .0001
    B. .0006
    C. .0036
    D. .0100

17. The sheet version of microfilm is NORMALLY referred to as 17._____
    A. microfiche
    B. micro-sheet
    C. microdupe
    D. microspec

18. While a line and staff organization is generally considered to have the advantages of both a line organization and a functional organization, with the disadvantages of each eliminated, disadvantages, nevertheless, do exist. 18._____
    Of the following, the one that describes the MOST significant disadvantage of a line and staff type of organization is that
    A. fewer opportunities are afforded to match the capacities of personnel with the job, since a smaller number of jobs is required
    B. line orders and staff advice, although clearly known to managers, tend to be confused by non-management members
    C. staff officers may attempt to take over line authority
    D. staff officers may tend to follow the ideas of the line officers and not generate their own ideas

19. Which activities take the most time? Are skills being utilized properly? Are employees doing too many unrelated tasks?
Of the following, the BEST technique to find answers to all of these questions is the 19.____
   A. flow diagram
   B. skills chart
   C. work count
   D. work distribution chart

20. Operator participation in management improvement work is LEAST likely to do which one of the following? 20.____
   A. Assure the use of the best available management techniques
   B. Make installation of new procedures quicker and easier
   C. Overcome the stigma of the outside expert
   D. Take advantage of the desire of most operators to seek self-improvement

21. Which of the following BEST defines an organization chart? A 21.____
   A. chart depicting the informal channels of communications within an organization
   B. chart depicting the major functions of an organization and the normal work flow between subdivisions of the organization
   C. graphic presentation of the arrangement and interrelationships of the subdivisions and functions of an organization as they exist
   D. graphic presentation of the arrangement and relationships of al positions authorized in an organization

22. Under a PPBS system, fiscal planning is NORMALLY considered to be planning 22.____
   A. for anticipated fixed costs only
   B. for present personnel requirements, procurement, and construction
   C. of current income and expenditures
   D. of future budgets

23. In the selection of space within an office building, LEAST consideration, generally, should be given to which of the following factors? 23.____
   A. Future expansion
   B. Proximity to elevators and restrooms
   C. Stability of other tenants on other floors
   D. Ventilation

24. In office layout, an office unit consisting of a combined desk and file cabinet and small movable partitions may BEST be described as _____ unit. 24.____
   A. conference
   B. landscaped office
   C. modular office
   D. semi-private office

25. Which of the following is it generally MOST important to consider when allocating office space? 25.____
   A. Actual organizational relationships
   B. Lighting requirements
   C. Noise levels
   D. Preferences of employees with over ten years of seniority

26. In preparing office layouts, the one of the following general factors within the affected unit which should generally receive the LEAST consideration is 26.____
   A. lighting levels in the existing area
   B. major work flow—the processing of paper
   C. present and projected growth rate of the unit
   D. traffic patterns of employees and visitors

27. In reviewing a new office layout, the one of the following questions that should normally receive LEAST consideration is: 27.____
   A. Have several alternate move day plans been prepared showing possible new locations of each piece of office equipment?
   B. Has expansion been provided for?
   C. Have alternate schemes been adequately explored to try to achieve the best possible layout?
   D. Is there adequate aisle space for ingress and egress?

28. Which of the following is the LEAST important reason for preparing a written study report? The 28.____
   A. report documents findings and recommendations so that the client can review and comment on them
   B. report is of interest as an historical document
   C. report serves as a document useful in implementing the recommendations
   D. writing process itself helps the analyst structure his thinking and conclusions

29. According to the classic studies by Rensis Likert at the University of Michigan, the GREATEST factor making for good morale and increased productivity was having a 29.____
   A. good program of employee benefits and wage scales
   B. supervisor who gave his employees free rein, after they were fully trained, and did not interfere with them
   C. supervisor who was interested primarily in production
   D. supervisor who, while also interested in production, was primarily "employee-centered"

30. Organization structure deals with the relationship of functions and the personnel performing these functions. It is usually advisable to think first of functions, then of the individuals performing these functions. 30.____
   MOST implicit in this approach is the recognition that
   A. conditions outside the organization may necessitate changes in the organization structure
   B. functions need not always be coordinated for an organization to effectively carry out its objectives
   C. functions tend to change with time while the interests and abilities of personnel are usually permanent
   D. personnel emphasis often results in unusual combinations of duties that are difficult to manage

KEY (CORRECT ANSWERS)

1.	D	11.	B	21.	C
2.	A	12.	C	22.	D
3.	C	13.	C	23.	C
4.	B	14.	A	24.	C
5.	B	15.	D	25.	A
6.	C	16.	B	26.	A
7.	D	17.	A	27.	A
8.	B	18.	C	28.	B
9.	B	19.	D	29.	D
10.	A	20.	A	30.	D

EXAMINATION SECTION

TEST 1

DIRECTIONS: Each question or incomplete statement is followed by several suggested answers or completions. Select the one that BEST answers the question or completes the statement. *PRINT THE LETTER OF THE CORRECT ANSWER IN THE SPACE AT THE RIGHT.*

1. In organizational theory, the optimum span of control, that is, the number of subordinates who can be effectively supervised by one man above the level of the first line supervisor is GENERALLY set at between 1.____
   A. 3 and 6 B. 6 and 12 C. 12 and 18 D. 18 and 24

2. Which of the following is LEAST desirable as a basic guide to normal conventional office layout? 2.____
   A. Arrange desks so that work flows in a normal fashion
   B. Place files nearest to the persons who will use them
   C. Utilize a number of small areas to provide privacy
   D. Utilize one single large area

3. *A set of objects together with relationships between the objects and between their attributes* is the definition of 3.____
   A. a perceptual whole and its subcomponents
   B. a system in the terms of specific systems theory
   C. an organism
   D. forms control

4. A technique of time study in which each employee maintains a record of his own time is GENERALLY known as _____ study. 4.____
   A. estimated time B. observed time
   C. time log D. wristwatch

5. An employee has approached a supervisor with a request for a change involving his personal status or with a suggestion for making an improvement in the work The supervisor knows that the suggestion cannot be granted. 5.____
   Of the following, the BEST procedure would be for the supervisor to
   A. refer the matter to the personnel department
   B. refer the matter to his superior for action
   C. reject the proposal, explaining the defects or objections which cannot be overcome
   D. shelve the idea so that the employee will realize it cannot be acted upon

6. There are, in general, a number of common methods of drawing samples for statistical work. 6.____
   The method in which a regularly ordered interval is maintained between the items chosen is BEST termed _____ sampling.
   A. random B. stratified or selective
   C. systematic D. work

7. The multi-column process chart can be put to all of the following general uses EXCEPT to 7.____
   A. improve office layout
   B. improve procedures
   C. standardize procedures
   D. train personnel

8. If one wished to show the percentage of change over a period of time, the MOST appropriate type of graph or chart GENERALLY would be the _____ chart. 8.____
   A. bar
   B. line or curve
   C. logarithmic or semilogarithmic
   D. pie

9. A chart designed for the explicit purpose of portraying graphically information relating to the degree of responsibility of key individuals for the performance of various functions is BEST described as a(n) _____ chart. 9.____
   A. linear responsibility
   B. work distribution
   C. work process
   D. staff

10. The technique of work measurement LEAST useful for setting up a program of office incentive pay GENERALLY would be 10.____
    A. log sheets
    B. stopwatch time study
    C. wristwatch time study
    D. work sampling

11. There are a number of steps to be taken in making a work sampling study in order to set production standards. Three of the steps listed below are peculiar only to work sampling, in contrast with other work measurement techniques. 11.____
    The one EXCEPTION is:
    A. Define the breakdown of work into the proper elements of work and no-work or delay to be observed
    B. Determine the required number of observations needed for the specified degree of reliability
    C. Establish the observation intervals
    D. Make a preliminary estimate of work and no-work or delay element percentages for step A

12. A number of standardized flow process chart symbols have been generally accepted. 12.____
    The symbol ⊽ GENERALLY indicates a(n)
    A. delay
    B. storage or file
    C. inspection
    D. operation

13. The number of standardized flow process chart symbols have been generally accepted. 13.____
    The symbol ▭ GENERALLY indicates a(n)
    A. delay
    B. storage or file
    C. inspection
    D. operation

14. The type of work for which short interval scheduling generally would be LEAST applicable would be the work of a group of 14.____
   A. calculating clerks B. order clerks
   C. technically-oriented clerks D. typists

15. In writing a business report, the BEST expression to use, in general, of those listed below would NORMALLY be: 15.____
   A. Because B. Inasmuch as
   C. In view of the fact that D. With reference to

16. Of the following, the MAJOR advantage of a random access data processing system, as compared with a sequential-type system, is its 16.____
   A. ability to use more than one input system
   B. demand for more sophisticated systems and programming
   C. greater storage capacity and access speed
   D. potential for processing data on a *first come, first-served* basis

17. A good rule to remember with regard to decision making is that decisions should be made 17.____
   A. at the highest level competent to make such a decision
   B. at the lowest level competent to make such a decision
   C. by the person responsible for carrying out the decision
   D. by the person responsible for the work of the unit

18. Which of the following potential systems would LEAST likely be improved by being online? A(n) _____ system. 18.____
   A. budgeting control B. welfare eligibility
   C. employee payroll D. inventory control

19. A management information and control system essentially should be designed to provide management personnel with up-to-date information which will enable them to improve control over their operations. 19.____
   In designing such a system, the FIRST step to determine is:
   A. What information is needed to effectively control operations?
   B. What information is presently available?
   C. What organization changes are necessary to implement the system?
   D. Who is presently processing the information that might be used?

20. In designing control reports, which of the following guidelines is of MOST importance? 20.____
   A. Financial information should always be carried to the nearest penny.
   B. The report should be a simple and concise statement of only the pertinent facts.
   C. The report should indicate the source of original data and how the computations were made.
   D. The report should have the broadest possible distribution at all levels of management.

21. A situation which enables a number of users at offsite locations to have access to an office computer network is called 21.____
   A. multiprocessing
   B. multiprogramming
   C. cloud connectivity
   D. remote access

22. Computer software that would typically be used for widespread dissemination of a business report is 22.____
   A. Microsoft Word
   B. Microsoft PowerPoint
   C. Adobe Elements
   D. Google Sheets

23. Which of the following steps is LEAST desirable in designing an electronic data processing system? 23.____
   A. Design the EDP system first, then relate it to current operations
   B. Develop a corollary chart for the corresponding flow of information
   C. Develop a flow chart for the functions affected by the system
   D. Obtain from available EDP equipment that which best fits current operations

24. Electronic data processing equipment can produce more information faster than can be generated by any other means. Because this is true, one wonders whether our ability to generate information has not far outstripped our ability to assimilate it. 24.____
   In view of this, a PERSISTENT danger management faces is in
   A. determining the budget for management information systems
   B. determining what information is of real worth
   C. finding enough computer personnel
   D. keeping their computers fully occupied

25. The one of the following that is an ADVANTAGE of a hybrid local/remote network setup over fully local access is 25.____
   A. the ability to access a network outside normal circumstances
   B. closer oversight of personnel
   C. more efficient workflow
   D. reduced costs for software and production equipment

KEY (CORRECT ANSWERS)

1.	A	11.	A
2.	C	12.	B
3.	A	13.	C
4.	C	14.	C
5.	C	15.	A
6.	C	16.	D
7.	A	17.	B
8.	C	18.	C
9.	A	19.	A
10.	A	20.	B

21. D
22. A
23. A
24. B
25. A

TEST 2

DIRECTIONS: Each question or incomplete statement is followed by several suggested answers or completions. Select the one that BEST answers the question or completes the statement. *PRINT THE LETTER OF THE CORRECT ANSWER IN THE SPACE AT THE RIGHT.*

1. In analyzing data for the acquisition of new equipment, an analyst gathers the facts, analyzes them, and develops new procedures which will be required when the new equipment arrives. 1.____
Inn analyzing the factors involved, which one of the following is normally LEAST important in the evaluation of new equipment?
   A. Cost factors
   B. Layout and installation factors
   C. Production planning
   D. Operational experience of manufacturers of allied equipment

2. If an analyst is required to recommend the selection of a machine for an office operation, he can BEST judge the expected output of a particular machine by pursuing which of the following courses of action? 2.____
Obtain
   A. an actual test run of the machine in his office
   B. data from the manufacturer of the machine
   C. information on the percentage of working time the machine will be used
   D. the experience of actual users of similar machines elsewhere

3. Of the following, the BEST definition of records management is 3.____
   A. storage of all types of records at minimum expense
   B. planned control of all types of records
   C. storage of records for maximum accessibility
   D. systematic filing of all types of records

4. The one of the following which is NOT a primary objective of a records retention and disposal system is to 4.____
   A. assure appropriate preservation of records having permanent value
   B. dispose of records not warranting further preservation
   C. establish retention standards for archives
   D. provide an opportunity to use miniaturization

5. Of the following functions of management, the one which should NORMALLY precede the others is 5.____
   A. coordinating B. directing C. organizing D. planning

6. One of the more famous studies of organizations is called the Hawthorne study. 6.____
This work was one of the first to point out the importance of
   A. employee's benefit and retirement programs
   B. informal organization among employees
   C. job engineering
   D. styles of position classification

7. In organization theory, the type of position in which an individual is appointed to give technical aid to management on a particular problem area is generally BEST termed a(n) 7.____
   A. administrative assistant
   B. assistant to
   C. staff assistant
   D. staff specialist

8. In organizing, doing what works in the particular situation, with due regard to both short- and long-range objective, is BEST termed 8.____
   A. ambivalence
   B. authoritarianism
   C. decentralization
   D. pragmatism

9. If an effort were made to reduce the number of private offices in a new layout, the LEAST effective substitute in offering privacy would be the use of 9.____
   A. an open area with lower movable partitions or railings separating each individual
   B. conference rooms
   C. larger desks
   D. modular desk units

10. The term *administrative substation* NORMALLY refers to 10.____
   A. a work station handling a number of office services for an office organization
   B. a work station where middle level supervisors are located
   C. an office for handling management trainees
   D. the functions allocated to particular levels of administrative managers

11. An operations research technique which would be applied to determine the optimum number of window clerks or interviewers to have in an agency serving the public would MOST likely be the use of 11.____
   A. line of balance
   B. queuing theory
   C. simulation
   D. work sampling

12. A type of file which permits the operator to remain seated while the file can be moved backward and forward as required is BEST termed a _____ file. 12.____
   A. lateral
   B. movable
   C. reciprocating
   D. rotary

13. The technique of work measurement in which the analyst observes the work at random times of the day is BEST termed 13.____
   A. indirect observation
   B. logging
   C. ratio delay
   D. wristwatch

14. Examples of predetermined time systems generally should include all of the following EXCEPT 14.____
   A. Master Clerical Data
   B. Methods Time Measurement
   C. Short Interval Data
   D. Work Factor

15. A technique by which the supervisor or an assistant distributes a predetermined batch of work to the employee at periodic intervals of the day is generally BEST known as 15.____
   A. backlog control scheduling
   B. production control scheduling
   C. short interval schedule
   D. workload balancing

16. E. Wright Bakke defined his *fusion process* as: The 16.____
   A. work environment to some degree remakes the organization and the organization to some degree remakes the work environment
   B. fusing of the interests of both management and labor unions
   C. community of interest between first line supervisors and top management
   D. organization to some degree remakes the individual and the individual to some degree remakes the organization

17. A pamphlet on issues related to 2020s-era office setup would likely be titled 17.____
   A. Close Encounters: How Proximity Elevates Production
   B. How Connectivity Spurs Inspiration
   C. See Your Employees in a New Light With Open Floor Plans
   D. From A to Zoom: The Terminology of the Hybrid Workplace

18. In planning office space for a newly established bureau, it would usually be LEAST desirable to 18.____
   A. concentrate, rather than disperse, the chief sources of office noises
   B. design an office environment with the same brightness as the office desk
   C. designate as reception rooms, washrooms, and other service areas those areas that will receive lesser amounts of illumination than those areas in which private office work will be performed
   D. eliminate natural light in cases where it is not the major light source

19. A private office should be used when its use is dictated by facts and unbiased judgment. It should never be provided simply because requests and sometimes pressure have been brought to bear. 19.____
   Of the following reasons used to justify use of a private office, the one that requires the MOST care in determining whether a private office is actually warranted is
   A. an office has always been provided for a particular job
   B. prestige considerations
   C. the confidential nature of the work
   D. the work involves high concentration

20. Theoretically, an ideal organization structure can be set up for each enterprise. In actual practice, the ideal organization structure is seldom, if ever, obtained. 20.____
   Of the following, the one that normally is of LEAST influence in determining the organization structure is the
   A. existence of agreements and favors among members of the organization
   B. funds available
   C. opinions and beliefs of top executives
   D. tendency of management to discard established forms in favor of new forms

21. An IMPORTANT aspect to keep in mind during the decision-making process is that 21.____
    A. all possible alternatives for attaining goals should be sought out and considered
    B. considering various alternatives only leads to confusion
    C. once a decision has been made, it cannot be retracted
    D. there is only one correct method to reach any goal

22. Implementation of accountability requires 22.____
    A. a leader who will not hesitate to take punitive action
    B. an established system of communication from the bottom to the top
    C. explicit directives from leaders
    D. too much expense to justify it

23. Of the following, the MAJOR difference between systems and procedures analysis and work simplification is: 23.____
    A. The former complicates organizational routine and the latter simplifies it
    B. The former is objective and the latter is subjective
    C. The former generally utilizes expert advice and the latter is a *do-it-yourself* improvement by supervisors and workers
    D. There is no difference other than in name

24. Systems development is concerned with providing 24.____
    A. a specific set of work procedures
    B. an overall framework to describe general relationships
    C. definitions of particular organizational functions
    D. organizational symbolism

25. Organizational systems and procedures should be 25.____
    A. developed as problems arise as no design can anticipate adequately the requirements of an organization
    B. developed jointly by experts in systems and procedures and the people who are responsible for implementing them
    C. developed solely by experts in systems and procedures
    D. eliminated whenever possible to save unnecessary expense

KEY (CORRECT ANSWERS)

1. D
2. A
3. B
4. D
5. D

6. B
7. D
8. D
9. C
10. A

11. B
12. C
13. C
14. C
15. C

16. D
17. D
18. D
19. A
20. D

21. A
22. B
23. C
24. B
25. B

TEST 3

DIRECTIONS: Each question or incomplete statement is followed by several suggested answers or completions. Select the one that BEST answers the question or completes the statement. *PRINT THE LETTER OF THE CORRECT ANSWER IN THE SPACE AT THE RIGHT.*

1. The CHIEF danger of a decentralized control system is that 1.____
   A. excessive reports and communications will be generated
   B. problem areas may not be detected readily
   C. the expense will become routine
   D. this will result in too many *chiefs*

2. Of the following, management guides and controls clerical work PRINCIPALLY through 2.____
   A. close supervision and constant checking of personnel
   B. spot checking of clerical procedures
   C. strong sanctions for clerical supervisors
   D. the use of printed forms

3. Which of the following is MOST important before conducting fact-finding interviews? 3.____
   A. Becoming acquainted with all personnel to be interviewed
   B. Explaining the techniques you plan to use
   C. Explaining to the operating officials the purpose and scope of the study
   D. Orientation of the physical layout

4. Of the following, the one that is NOT essential in carrying out a comprehensive work improvement program is 4.____
   A. standards of performance
   B. supervisory training
   C. work count/task list
   D. work distribution chart

5. Which of the following control techniques is MOST useful on large complex systems projects? 5.____
   A. A general work plan
   B. Gantt chart
   C. Monthly progress report
   D. PERT chart

6. The action which is MOST effective in gaining acceptance of a study by the agency which is being studied is 6.____
   A. a directive from the agency head to install a study based on recommendations included in a report
   B. a lecture-type presentation following approval of the procedures
   C. a written procedure in narrative form covering the proposed system with visual presentations and discussions
   D. procedural charts showing the *before* situation, forms, steps, etc. to the employees affected

7. Which of the following is NOT an advantage in the use of oral instructions as compared with written instructions? Oral instruction(s) 7.____
   A. can easily be changed
   B. is superior in transmitting complex directives
   C. facilitate exchange of information between a superior and his subordinate
   D. with discussions make it easier to ascertain understanding

8. Which organization principle is MOST closely related to procedural analysis and improvement? 8.____
   A. Duplication, overlapping, and conflict should be eliminated.
   B. Managerial authority should be clearly defined.
   C. The objectives of the organization should be clearly defined.
   D. Top management should be freed of burdensome detail.

9. Which one of the following is the MAJOR objective of operational audits? 9.____
   A. Detecting fraud
   B. Determining organization problems
   C. Determining the number of personnel needed
   D. Recommending opportunities for improving operating and management practices

10. Of the following, the formalization of organization structure is BEST achieved by 10.____
    A. a narrative description of the plan of organization
    B. functional charts
    C. job descriptions together with organization charts
    D. multi-flow charts

11. Budget planning is MOST useful when it achieves 11.____
    A. cost control
    B. forecast of receipts
    C. performance review
    D. personnel reduction

12. The UNDERLYING principle of sound administration is to 12.____
    A. base administration on investigation facts
    B. have plenty of resources available
    C. hire a strong administrator
    D. establish a broad policy

13. Although questionnaires are not the best survey tool the management analyst has to use, there are times when a good questionnaire can expedite the *fact-finding* phase of a management survey. 13.____
    Which of the following should be AVOIDED in the design and distribution of the questionnaire?
    A. Questions should be framed so that answers can be classified and tabulated for analysis.
    B. Those receiving the questionnaire must be knowledgeable enough to accurately provide the information desired.

C. The questionnaire should enable the respondent to answer in a narrative manner.
D. The questionnaire should require a minimum amount of writing.

14. Of the following, the formula which is used to calculate the arithmetic mean from data grouped in a frequency distribution is M = 14.____

A. $\frac{N}{\Sigma fx}$ B. $N(\Sigma fx)$ C. $\frac{\Sigma fx}{N}$ D. $\frac{\Sigma x}{fN}$

15. Arranging large groups of numbers in frequency distributions 15.____
A. gives a more composite picture of the total group than a random listing
B. is misleading in most cases
C. is unnecessary in most instances
D. presents the data in a form whereby further manipulation of the group is eliminated

16. After a budget has been developed, it serves to 16.____
A. assist the accounting department in posting expenditures
B. measure the effectiveness of department managers
C. provide a yardstick against which actual costs are measured
D. provide the operating department with total expenditure to date

17. Of the following, which formula is used to determine staffing requirements? 17.____

A. $\frac{\text{Hours per man-day}}{\text{Volume x Standard}}$ = Employees Needed

B. $\frac{\text{Hours per man-day x Standard}}{\text{Volume}}$ = Employees Needed

C. $\frac{\text{Hours per man-day x Volume}}{\text{Standard}}$ = Employees Needed

D. $\frac{\text{Volume x Standard}}{\text{Hours per man-day}}$ = Employees Needed

18. Of the following, which formula is used to determine the number of days required to process work? 18.____

A. $\frac{\text{Employees x Daily Output}}{\text{Volume}}$ = Days to Process Work

B. $\frac{\text{Employees x Volume}}{\text{Daily Output}}$ = Days to Process Work

C. $\frac{\text{Volume}}{\text{Employees x Daily Output}}$ = Days to Process Work

D. $\frac{\text{Volume x Daily Output}}{\text{Employees}}$ = Days to Process Work

19. Identify this symbol, as used in a Systems Flow Chart. 19.____
    A. Document
    B. Decision
    C. Preparation
    D. Process

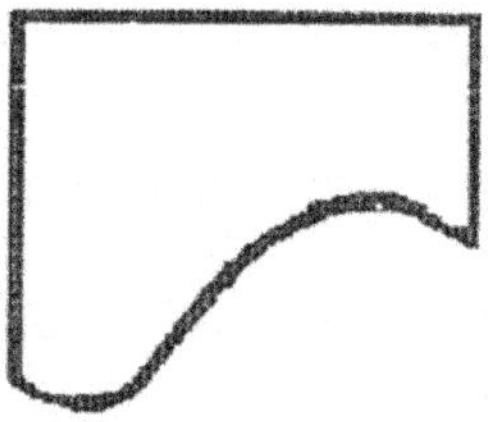

20. Of the following, the MAIN advantage of a form letter over a dictated letter is that a form letter 20.____
    A. is more expressive
    B. is neater
    C. may be mailed in a window envelope
    D. requires less secretarial time

21. The term that may be defined as a *systematic analysis of all factors affecting work being done or all factors that will affect work to be done, in order to save effort, time, or money* is 21.____
    A. flow process charting
    B. work flow analysis
    C. work measurement
    D. work simplification

22. Generally, the LEAST important basic factor to be considered in developing office layout improvements is to locate 22.____
    A. office equipment, reference facilities, and files as close as practicable to those using them
    B. persons as close as practicable to the persons from whom they receive their work
    C. persons as close as practicable to windows and/or adequate ventilation
    D. persons who are friendly with each other close together to improve morale

23. Of the following, the one which is LEAST effective in reducing administrative costs is 23.____
    A. applying objective measurement techniques to determine the time required to perform a given task
    B. establishing budgets on the basis of historical performance data
    C. motivating supervisors and managers in the importance of cost reduction
    D. selecting the best method—manual, mechanical, or electronic—to process the essential work

24. *Fire-fighting* is a common expression in management terminology. 24.____
    Of the following, which BEST describes *fire-fighting* as an analyst's approach to solving paperwork problems?
    A. A complete review of all phases of the department's processing functions
    B. A studied determination of the proper equipment to process the work
    C. An analysis of each form that is being processed and the logical reasons for its processing
    D. The solution of problems as they arise, usually at the request of operating personnel

25. Assume that an analyst with a proven record of accomplishment on many projects is having difficulties on his present assignment. 25.____
Of the following, the BEST course of action for his superior to take is to
   A. assume there is a personality conflict involved and transfer the analyst to another project
   B. give the analyst some time off
   C. review the nature of the project to determine whether or not the analyst is equipped to handle the assignment
   D. suggest that the analyst seek counseling

KEY (CORRECT ANSWERS)

1.	B	11.	A
2.	D	12.	A
3.	C	13.	C
4.	B	14.	C
5.	D	15.	A
6.	C	16.	C
7.	B	17.	D
8.	A	18.	C
9.	D	19.	A
10.	C	20.	D

21.	D
22.	D
23.	B
24.	D
25.	C

EXAMINATION SECTION

TEST 1

DIRECTIONS: Each question or incomplete statement is followed by several suggested answers or completions. Select the one that BEST answers the question or completes the statement. *PRINT THE LETTER OF THE CORRECT ANSWER IN THE SPACE AT THE RIGHT.*

1. An executive assigns A, the head of a staff unit, to devise plans for reducing the delay in submittal of reports by a local agency headed by C. The reports are under the supervision of C's subordinate line official B with whom A is to deal directly. In his investigation, A finds: (1) the reasons for the delay; and (2) poor practices which have either been overlooked or condoned by line official B. 1.____
   Of the following courses of action A could take, the BEST one would be to
   A. develop recommendations with line official B with regard to reducing the delay and correcting the poor practice and then report fully to his own executive
   B. discuss the findings with C in an attempt to correct the situation before making any formal report on the poor practices
   C. report both findings to his executive, attaching the explanation offered by C
   D. report to his executive on the first finding and discuss the second in a friendly way with line official B
   E. report the first finding to his executive, ignoring the second until his opinion is requested

2. Drafts of a proposed policy, prepared by a staff committee, are circulated to ten member of the field staff of the organization by route slips with a request for comments within two weeks. Two members of the field staff make extensive comments, four offer editorial suggestions, and the remainder make minor favorable comments. Shortly after, it found that the statement needs considerable revision by the field staff. 2.____
   Of the following possible reasons for the original failure of the field staff to identify difficulties, the MOST likely is that the
   A. field staff did not take sufficient time to review the manual
   B. field staff had not been advised of the type of contribution expected
   C. low morale of the field staff prevented their showing interest
   D. policy statement was too advanced for the staff
   E. staff committee was not sufficiently representative

3. Operator participation in management improvement work is LEAST likely to 3.____
   A. assure the use of best available management technique
   B. overcome the stigma of the outside expert
   C. place responsibility for improvement in the person who knows the job best
   D. simplify installation
   E. take advantage of the desire of most operators to seek self-improvement

4. In general, the morale of workers in an agency is MOST frequently and MOST significantly affected by the 4.____
   A. agency policies of organizational structure and operational procedures
   B. distance of the employee's job from his home community
   C. fringe benefits
   D. number of opportunities for advancement
   E. relationship with supervisors

5. Of the following, the PRIMARY function of a work distribution chart is to 5.____
   A. analyze the soundness of existing divisions of labor
   B. eliminate the unnecessary clerical detail
   C. establish better supervisory techniques
   D. simplify work methods
   E. weed out core functions

6. In analyzing a process chart, which one of the following should be asked FIRST? 6.____
   A. How B. When C. Where D. Who E. Why

7. Which one of the following is NOT an advantage of the interview method of collecting data? It 7.____
   A. enables interviewer to judge the person interviewed on such matters as general attitude, knowledge, etc.
   B. helps build up personal relations for later installation of changes
   C. is a flexible method that can be adjusted to changing circumstances
   D. permits the obtaining of *off the record* information
   E. produces more accurate information than other methods

8. Which one of the following may be defined as a *regularly recurring appraisal of the manner in which all elements of agency management are being carried out*? 8.____
   A. Functional survey
   B. Operations audit
   C. Organization survey
   D. Over-all survey
   E. Reconnaissance survey

9. An analysis of the flow of work in a department should begin with the _____ work. 9.____
   A. major routine
   B. minor routine
   C. supervisory
   D. technical
   E. unusual

10. Which method would MOST likely be used to get first-hand information on complaints from the public? 10.____
   A. Study of correspondence
   B. Study of work volume
   C. Tracing specific transactions through a series of steps
   D. Tracing use of forms
   E. Worker desk audit

11. People will generally produce the MOST if 11.____
    A. management exercises close supervision over the work
    B. there is strict discipline in the group
    C. they are happy in their work
    D. they feel involved in their work
    E. they follow *the one best way*

12. The normal analysis of which chart listed below is MOST closely related to organizational analysis? _____ chart. 12.____
    A. Layout B. Operation C. Process
    D. Work count E. Work distribution

13. The work count would be LEAST helpful in accomplishing which one of the following? 13.____
    A. Demonstrating personnel needs B. Improving the sequence of steps
    C. Measuring the value of a step D. Spotting bottlenecks
    E. Stimulating interest in work

14. Which one of the following seems LEAST useful as a guide in interviewing an employee in a procedure and methods survey? 14.____
    A. Explaining who you are and the purpose of your visit
    B. Having a general plan of what you intend to get from the interview
    C. Listening carefully and not interrupting
    D. Trying out his reactions to your ideas for improvements
    E. Trying to analyze his reasons for saying what he says

15. Which one of the following is an advantage of the questionnaire method of gathering facts as compared with the interview method? 15.____
    A. Different people may interpret the questions differently
    B. Less *off the record* information is given
    C. More time may be taken in order to give exact answers
    D. Personal relationships with the people involved are not established
    E. There is less need for follow-up

16. Which one of the following is generally NOT an advantage of the personal observation method of gathering facts? It 16.____
    A. enables staff to use *off the record* information if personally observed
    B. helps in developing valid recommendations
    C. helps the person making the observation acquire *know how* valuable for later installation and follow-up
    D. is economical in time and money
    E. may turn up other problems in need of solution

17. Which of the following would MOST often be the best way to minimize resistance to change? 17.____
    A. Break the news about the change gently to the people affected
    B. Increase the salary of the people affected by the change
    C. Let the people concerned participate at the decision to change

D. Notify all people concerned with the change, both orally and in writing
E. Stress the advantages of the new system

18. The functional organization chart 18.____
    A. does not require periodic revision
    B. includes a description of the duties of each organization segment
    C. includes positions and titles for each organization segment
    D. is the simplest type of organization chart
    E. is used primarily by newly established agencies

19. The principle of span of control has frequently been said to be in conflict with the 19.____
    A. principle of unity of command
    B. principle that authority should be commensurate with responsibility
    C. principle that like functions should be grouped into one unit
    D. principle that the number of levels between the top of an organization and the bottom should be small
    E. scalar principle

20. If an executive delegates to his subordinates authority to handle problems of a routine nature for which standard solutions have been established, he may expect that 20.____
    A. fewer complaint will be received
    B. he has made it more difficult for his subordinates to solve these problems
    C. he has opened the way for confusion in his organization
    D. there will be a lack of consistency in the methods applied to the solution of these problems
    E. these routine problems will be handled efficiently and he will have more time for other non-routine work

21. Which of the following would MOST likely be achieved by a change in the basic organization structure from the *process* or *functional* type to the *purpose* or *product* type? 21.____
    A. Easier recruitment of personnel in a tight labor market
    B. Fixing responsibility at a lower level in the organization
    C. Greater centralization
    D. Greater economy
    E. Greater professional development

22. Usually the MOST difficult problem in connection with a major reorganization is 22.____
    A. adopting a pay plan to fit the new structure
    B. bringing the organization manual up-to-date
    C. determining the new organization structure
    D. gaining acceptance of the new plan by the higher level employees
    E. gaining acceptance of the new plan by the lower level employees

23. Which of the following statements MOST accurately describes the work of the chiefs of MOST staff divisions in departments? 23.____
Chiefs
    A. focus more on getting the job done than on how it is done
    B. are mostly interested in short-range results
    C. nearly always advise but rarely advise
    D. usually command or control but rarely advise
    E. provide service to the rest of the organization and/or assist the chief executive in planning and controlling operations

24. In determining the type of organization structure of an enterprise, the one factor that might be given relatively greater weight in a small organization than in a larger organization of the same nature is the 24.____
    A. geographical location of the enterprise
    B. individual capabilities of incumbents
    C. method of financing to be employed
    D. size of the area served
    E. type of activity engaged in

25. Functional foremanship differs MOST markedly from generally accepted principle of administration in that it advocates 25.____
    A. an unlimited span of control
    B. less delegation of responsibility
    C. more than one supervisor for an employee
    D. nonfunctional organization
    E. substitution of execution for planning

KEY (CORRECT ANSWERS)

1. A
2. B
3. A
4. E
5. A

6. E
7. E
8. B
9. A
10. A

11. D
12. E
13. B
14. D
15. C

16. D
17. C
18. B
19. D
20. E

21. B
22. D
23. E
24. B
25. C

TEST 2

DIRECTIONS: Each question or incomplete statement is followed by several suggested answers or completions. Select the one that BEST answers the question or completes the statement. *PRINT THE LETTER OF THE CORRECT ANSWER IN THE SPACE AT THE RIGHT.*

1. Decentralization of the authority to make decisions is a necessary result of increased complexity in an organization, but for the sake of efficiency and coordination of operations, such decentralization must be planned carefully. A good general rule is that 1.____
   A. any decision should be made at the lowest possible point in the organization where all the information and competence necessary for a sound decision are available
   B. any decision should be made at the highest possible point in the organization, thus guaranteeing the best decision
   C. any decision should be made at the lowest possible point in the organization, but always approved by management
   D. any decision should be made by management and referred to the proper subordinate for comment
   E. no decision should be made by any individual in the organization without approval by a superior

2. One drawback of converting a conventional consecutive filing system to a terminal digit filing system for a large installation is that 2.____
   A. conversion would be expensive in time and manpower
   B. conversion would prevent the proper use of recognized numeric classification systems, such as the Dewey decimal, in classifying files material
   C. responsibility for proper filing cannot be pinpointed in the terminal digit system
   D. the terminal digit system requires considerably more space than a normal filing system

3. The basic filing system that would ordinarily be employed in a large administrative headquarters unit is the _____ file system. 3.____
   A alphabetic
   B. chronological
   C. mnemonic
   D. retention
   E. subject classification

4. A records center is of benefit in a records management program PRIMARILY because 4.____
   A. all the records of the organization are kept in one place
   B. inactive records can be stored economically in less expense storage areas
   C. it provides a place where useless records can be housed at little or no cost to the organization

D. obsolete filing and storage equipment can be utilized out of view of the public
E. records analysts can examine an organization's files without affecting the unit's operation or upsetting the supervisors

5. In examining a number of different forms to see whether any could be combined or eliminated, which of the following would one be MOST likely to use? 5.____
A. Forms analysis sheet of recurring data
B. Forms control log
C. Forms design and approval request
D. Forms design and guide sheet
E. Numerical file

6. The MOST important reason for control of *bootleg* forms is that 6.____
A. they are more expensive than authorized forms
B. they are usually poorly designed
C. they can lead to unnecessary procedures
D. they cannot be reordered as easily as authorized terms
E. violation of rules and regulations should not be allowed

7. With a box design of a form, the caption title or question to be answered should be located in the _____ of the box. 7.____
A. center at the bottom
B. center at the top
C. lower left corner
D. lower right corner
E. upper left corner

8. A two-part snapout form would be MOST properly justified if 8.____
A. it is a cleaner operation
B. it is prepared ten times a week
C. it saves time in preparation
D. it is to be filled out by hand rather than by typewriter
E. proper registration is critical

9. When deciding whether or not to approve a request for a new form, which reference is normally MOST pertinent? 9.____
A. Alphabetical Forms File
B. Functional Forms File
C. Numerical Forms File
D. Project Completion Report
E. Records Retention Data

10. Which of the following statements BEST explains the significance of the famed Hawthorne Plant experiments? 10.____
They showed that
A. a large span of control leads to more production than a small span of control
B. morale has no relationship to production
C. personnel counseling is of relatively little importance in a going organization

D. the special attention received by a group in an experimental situation has a greater impact on production than changes in working conditions
E. there is a direct relationship between the amount of illumination and production

11. Which of the following would most often NOT result from a highly efficient management control system? 11.____
A. Facilitation of delegation
B. Highlighting of problem areas
C. Increase in willingness of people to experiment or to take calculated risks
D. Provision of an objective test of new ideas or new methods and procedures
E. Provision of information useful for revising objectives, programs, and operations

12. The PERT system is a 12.____
A. method for laying out office space on a modular basis utilizing prefabricated partitions
B. method of motivating personnel to be continuously alert and to improve their appearance
C. method of program planning and control using a network or flow plan
D. plan for expanding reporting techniques
E. simplified method of cost accounting

13. The term *management control* is MOST frequently used to mean 13.____
A. an objective and unemotional approach by management
B. coordinating the efforts of all parts of the organization
C. evaluation of results in relation to plan
D. giving clear, precise orders to subordinates
E. keeping unions from making managerial decisions

14. Which one of the following factors has the MOST bearing on the frequency with which a control report should be made? 14.____
A. Degree of specialization of the work
B. Degree of variability in activities
C. Expense of the report
D. Number of levels of supervision
E. Number of personnel involved

15. The value of statistical records is MAINLY dependent upon the 15.____
A. method of presenting the material
B. number of items used
C. range of cases sampled
D. reliability of the information used
E. time devoted to compiling the material

16. When a supervisor delegates an assignment, he should 16.____
   A. delegate his responsibility for the assignment
   B. make certain that the assignment is properly performed
   C. participate in the beginning and final stages of the assignment
   D. retail all authority needed to complete the assignment
   E oversee all stages of the assignment

17. Assume that the department in which you are employed has never given official sanction to a mid-afternoon coffee break. Some bureaus have it and others do not. In the latter case, some individuals merely absent themselves for about 15 minutes at 3 P.M. while others remain on the job despite the fatigue which seems to be common among all employees in this department at that time. 17.____
   The course of action which you should recommend, if possible, is to
   A. arrange a schedule of mid-afternoon coffee breaks for all employees
   B. forbid all employees to take a mid-afternoon coffee break
   C. permit each bureau to decide for itself whether or not it will have a coffee break
   D. require all employees who wish a coffee break to take a shorter lunch period
   E. arrange a poll to discover the consensus of the department

18. The one of the following which is LEAST important in the management of a suggestion program is 18.____
   A. giving awards which are of sufficient value to encourage competition
   B. securing full support from the department's officers and executives
   C. publicizing the program and the awards given
   D. holding special conferences to analyze and evaluate some of the suggestions needed
   E. providing suggestion boxes in numerous locations

19. The one of the following which is MOST likely to decrease morale is 19.____
   A. insistence on strict adherence to safety rules
   B. making each employee responsible for the tidiness of his work area
   C. overlooking evidence of hostility between groups of employees
   D. strong, aggressive leadership
   E. allocating work on the basis of personal knowledge of the abilities and interests of the member of the department

20. Assume that a certain office procedure has been standard practice for many years. 20.____
   When a new employee asks why this particular procedure is followed, the supervisor should FIRST
   A. explain that everyone does it that way
   B. explain the reason for the procedure
   C. inform him that it has always been done that way in that particular office
   D. tell him to try it for a while before asking questions
   E. tell him he has never thought about it that way

21. Several employees complain informally to their supervisor regarding some new procedures which have been instituted. 21.____
The supervisor should IMMEDIATELY
   A. explain that management is responsible
   B. state frankly that he had nothing to do with it
   C. refer the matter to the methods analyst
   D. tell the employees to submit their complaint as a formal grievance
   E. investigate the complaint

22. A new employee asks his supervisor how he is doing. Actually, he is not doing well in some phases of the job, but it is felt that he will learn in time. 22.____
The BEST response for the supervisor to make is:
   A. Some things you are doing well, and in others I am sure you will improve.
   B. Wait until the end of your probation period when we will discuss this matter.
   C. You are not doing too well.
   D. You are doing very well.
   E. I'll be able to tell you when I go over your record.

23. The PRINCIPAL aim of a supervisor is to 23.____
   A. act as liaison between employee and management
   B. get the work done
   C. keep up morale
   D. train his subordinates
   E. become chief of the department

24. When the work of two bureaus must be coordinated, direct contact between the subordinates in each bureau who are working on the problem is 24.____
   A. *bad*, because it violates the chain of command
   B. *bad*, because they do not have authority to make decisions
   C. *good*, because it enable quicker results
   D. *good*, because it relieves their superiors of any responsibilities
   E. *bad*, because they may work at cross purposes

25. Of the following, the organization defect which can be ascertained MOST readily merely by analyzing an accurate and well-drawn organization chart is 25.____
   A. ineffectiveness of an activity
   B. improper span of control
   C. inappropriate assignment of functions
   D. poor supervision
   E. unlawful delegation of authority

KEY (CORRECT ANSWERS)

1. A
2. A
3. E
4. B
5. A

6. C
7. E
8. E
9. B
10. D

11. C
12. C
13. C
14. B
15. D

16. B
17. A
18. E
19. C
20. B

21. E
22. A
23. B
24. C
25. B

EXAMINATION SECTION

TEST 1

DIRECTIONS: Each question or incomplete statement is followed by several suggested answers or completions. Select the one that BEST answers the question or completes the statement. *PRINT THE LETTER OF THE CORRECT ANSWER IN THE SPACE AT THE RIGHT.*

1. A management approach widely used today is based on the belief that decisions should be made and actions should be taken by managers closest to the organization's problems. 1.____
   This style of management is MOST appropriately called _____ management.
   A. scientific
   B. means-end
   C. decentralized
   D. internal process

2. As contrasted with tall organization structures with narrow spans of control, flat organization structures with wide spans of control MOST usually provide 2.____
   A. fast communication and information flows
   B. more levels in the organizational hierarchy
   C. fewer workers reporting to supervisors
   D. lower motivation because of tighter control standards

3. Use of the systems approach is MOST likely to lead to 3.____
   A. consideration of the impact on the whole organization of actions taken in any part of that organization
   B. the placing of restrictions on departmental activity
   C. use of mathematical models to suboptimize production
   D. consideration of the activities of each unit of an organization as a totality without regard to the remainder of the organization

4. An administrator, with overall responsibility for all administrative operations in a large operating agency, is considering organizing the agency's personnel office around either of the following two alternative concepts: 4.____
   Alternative I: A corps of specialists for each branch of personnel subject matter, whose skills, counsel, or work products are coordinated only by the agency personnel officer
   Alternative II: A crew of so-called *personnel generalists*, who individually work with particular segments of the organization but deal with all subspecialties of the personnel function
   The one of the following which MOST tends to be a DRAWBACK of Alternative I, as compared with Alternative II, is that
   A. training and employee relations work call for education, interests, and talents that differ from those required for classification and compensation work
   B. personnel office staff may develop only superficial familiarity with the specialized areas to which they have been assigned

C. supervisors may fail to get continuing overall personnel advice on an integrated basis
D. the personnel specialists are likely to become so interested in and identified with the operating view as to particular cases that they lose their professional objectivity and become merely advocates of what some supervisor wants

5. The matrix summary or decision matrix is a useful tool for making choices. Its effectiveness is MOST dependent upon the user's ability to 5.____
A. write a computer program (Fortran or Cobol)
B. assign weights representing the relative importance of the objectives
C. solve a set of two equations with two unknowns
D. work with matrix algebra

6. An organizational form which is set up only on an *ad hoc* basis to meet specific goals is said PRIMARILY to use 6.____
A. clean break departmentation
B. matrix or task force organization
C. scalar specialization
D. geographic or area-wide decentralization

7. The concept of job enlargement would LEAST properly be implemented by 7.____
A. permitting workers to follow through on tasks or projects from start to finish
B. delegating the maximum authority possible for decision-making to lower levels in the hierarchy
C. maximizing the number of professional classes in the classification plan
D. training employees to grow beyond whatever tasks they have been performing

8. As used in the area of admission, the principle of *unity of command* MOST specifically means that 8.____
A. an individual should report to only one superior for any single activity
B. individuals make better decisions than do committees
C. in large organizations, chains of command are normally too long
D. an individual should not supervise over five subordinates

9. The method of operations research, statistical decision-making, and linear programming have been referred to as the tool kit of the manager. Utilization of these tools is LEAST useful in the performance of which of the following functions? 9.____
A. Elimination of the need for using judgment when making decisions
B. Facilitation of decision-making without the need for sub-optimization
C. Quantifying problems for management study
D. Research and analysis of management operations

10. When acting in their respective managerial capacities, the chief executive officer and the office supervisor both perform the fundamental functions of management. 10.____
Of the following differences between the two, the one which is generally considered to be the LEAST significant is the
   A. breadth of the objectives
   B. complexity of measuring actual efficiency of performance
   C. number of decisions made
   D. organizational relationships affected by actions taken

11. The ability of operations researchers to solve complicated problems rests on their use of models. 11.____
These models can BEST be described as
   A. mathematical statements of the problem
   B. physical constructs that simulate a work layout
   C. toy-like representations of employees in work environments
   D. role-playing simulations

12. Of the following, it is MOST likely to be proper for the agency head to allow the agency personnel officer to make final selection of appointees from certified eligible lists where there are 12.____
   A. *small* numbers of employees to be hired in newly-developed professional fields
   B. *large* numbers of persons to be hired for key managerial positions
   C. *large* numbers of persons to be hired in very routine occupations where the individual discretion of operating officials is not vital
   D. *small* numbers of persons to be hired in highly specialized professional occupations which are vital to the agency's operations

13. Of the following, an operating agency personnel office is LEAST likely to be able to exert strong influence or control within the operating agency by 13.____
   A. interpreting to the operating agency head what is intended by the directives and rules emanating from the central personnel agency
   B. establishing the key objectives of those line divisions of the operating agency employing large numbers of staff and operating under the management-by-objectives approach
   C. formulating and proposing to the agency head the internal policies and procedures on personnel matters required within the operating agency
   D. exercising certain discretionary authority in the application of the agency head's general personnel policies to actual specific situations

14. PERT is a recently developed system used PRIMARILY to 14.____
   A. evaluate the quality of applicants' background
   B. analyze and control the timing aspects of a major project
   C. control the total expenditure of agency funds within a monthly or quarterly time period
   D. analyze and control the differential effect on costs of purchasing different quantities

15. Assume that an operating agency has among its vacant positions two positions, each of which encompasses mixed duties. Both require appointees to have considerable education and experience, but these requirements are essential only for the more difficult duties of these positions. In the place of these positions, an administrator creates two new positions, one in which the higher duties are concentrated and the other with the lesser functions requiring only minimum preparation. 15.____
Of the following, it is generally MOST appropriate to characterize the administrator's action as a(n)
   A. *undesirable* example of deliberate downgrading of standards and requirements
   B. *undesirable* manipulation of the classification system for non-merit purposes
   C. *desirable* broadening of the definition of a class of positions
   D. *desirable* example of job redesign

16. Of the following, the LEAST important stumbling block to the development of personnel mobility among governmental jurisdictions is the 16.____
   A. limitations on lateral entry above junior levels in many jurisdictions
   B. continued collection of filing fees for civil service tests by many governmental jurisdictions
   C. absence of reciprocal exchange of retirement benefit eligibility between governments
   D. disparities in salary scales between governments

17. Of the following, the MAJOR disadvantage of a personnel system that features the *selection out* (forced retirement) of those who have been passed over a number of times for promotion is that such a system 17.____
   A. wastes manpower which is perfectly competent at one level but unable to rise above that level
   B. wastes funds by requiring review boards
   C. leads to excessive recruiting of newcomers from outside the system
   D. may not be utilized in *closed* career systems with low maximum age limits for entrance

18. Of the following, the fields in which operating agency personnel offices generally exercise the MOST stringent controls over first line supervisors in the agency are 18.____
   A. methods analysis and work simplification
   B. selection and position classification
   C. vestibule training and Gantt chart
   D. suggestion systems and staff development

19. Of the following, computers are normally MOST effective in handling 19.____
   A. large masses of data requiring simple processing
   B. small amounts of data requiring constantly changing complex processing
   C. data for which reported values are often subject to inaccuracies
   D. large amounts of data requiring continual programming and reprocessing

20. Contingency planning, which has long been used by the military and is assuming increasing importance in other organizations, may BEST be described as a process which utilizes 20.____
   A. alternative plans based on varying assumptions
   B. *crash programs* by organizations departmentalized along process lines
   C. plans which mandate substitution of equipment for manpower at predetermined operational levels
   D. plans that individually and accurately predict future events

21. In the management of inventory, two kinds of costs normally determine when to order and in what amounts. 21.____
The one of the following choices which includes BOTH of these kinds of costs is _____ costs and _____ costs.
   A. carrying; storage
   B. personnel; order
   C. computer; order
   D. personnel; computer

22. At top management levels, the one of the following which is generally the MOST important executive skill is skill in 22.____
   A. budgeting procedures
   B. a technical discipline
   C. controlling actions in accordance with previously approved plans
   D. seeing the organization as a whole

23. Of the following, the BEST way to facilitate the successful operation of a committee is to set guidelines establishing its 23.____
   A. budget exclusive of personnel costs
   B. location
   C. schedule of meetings or conferences
   D. scope of purpose

24. Executive training programs that single out particular managers and groom them for promotion create the so-called organizational *crown princes*. 24.____
Of the following, the MOST serious problem that arises in connection with this practice is that
   A. the managers chosen for promotion seldom turn out to be the best managers since the future potential of persons cannot be predicted
   B. not enough effort is made to remove organizational obstacles in the way of their development and achievement
   C. the resentment of the managers not selected for the program has an adverse effect on the motivation of those managers not selected
   D. performance appraisal and review are not carried out systematically enough

25. Of the following, the LEAST likely result of the use of the concept of job enlargement is that 25.____
   A. coordination will be simplified
   B. the individual's job will become less challenging
   C. worker satisfaction will increase
   D. fewer people will have to give attention to each piece of work

KEY (CORRECT ANSWERS)

1. C
2. A
3. A
4. C
5. B

6. B
7. C
8. A
9. A
10. C

11. A
12. C
13. B
14. B
15. D

16. B
17. A
18. B
19. A
20. A

21. A
22. D
23. D
24. C
25. B

TEST 2

DIRECTIONS: Each question or incomplete statement is followed by several suggested answers or completions. Select the one that BEST answers the question or completes the statement. *PRINT THE LETTER OF THE CORRECT ANSWER IN THE SPACE AT THE RIGHT.*

1. The one of the following which is MOST likely to be emphasized in the use of the brainstorming technique is the 1.____
   A. early consideration of cost factors of all ideas which may be suggested
   B. avoidance of impractical suggestions
   C. separation of the generation of ideas from their evaluation
   D. appraisal of suggestions concurrently with their initial presentation

2. Of the following, the BEST method for assessing managerial performance is generally to 2.____
   A. compare the manager's accomplishments against clear, specific, agreed-upon goals
   B. compare the manager's traits with those of his peers on a predetermined objective
   C. measure the manager's behavior against a listing of itemized personal traits
   D. measure the manager's success according to the enumeration of the *satisfaction* principle

3. As compared with recruitment from outside, selection from within the service must generally show GREATER concern for the 3.____
   A. prestige in which the public service as a whole is held by the public
   B. morale of the candidate group compromising the recruitment field
   C. cost of examining per candidate
   D. benefits of the use of standardized and validated tests

4. Performance budgeting focuses PRIMARY attention upon which one of the following? The 4.____
   A. things to be acquired, such as supplies and equipment
   B. general character and relative importance of the work to be done or the service to be rendered
   C. list of personnel to be employed, by specific title
   D. separation of employee performance evaluations from employee compensation

5. Of the following, the FIRST step in the installation and operation of a performance budgeting system generally should be the 5.____
   A. identification of program costs in relationship to the accounting system and operating structure
   B. identification of the specific end results of past programs in other jurisdictions

C. identification of work programs that are meaningful for management purposes
D. establishment of organizational structures each containing only one work program

6. Of the following, the MOST important purpose of a system of quarterly allotments of appropriated funds generally is to enable the 6.____
A. head of the judicial branch to determine the legality of agency requests for budget increases
B. operating agencies of government to upgrade the quality of their services without increasing costs
C. head of the executive branch to control the rate at which the operating agencies obligate and expend funds
D. operating agencies of government to avoid payment for services which have not been properly rendered by employees

7. In the preparation of the agency's budget, the agency's central budget office has two responsibilities: program review and management improvement. 7.____
Which one of the following questions concerning an operating agency's program is MOST closely related to the agency budget officer's program review responsibility?
A. Can expenditures for supplies, materials, or equipment be reduced?
B. Will improved work methods contribute to a more effective program?
C. What is the relative importance of this program as compared to a higher level of program performance?
D. Will a realignment of responsibilities contribute to a higher level of program performance?

8. Of the following, the method of evaluating relative rates of return normally and generally thought to be MOST useful in evaluating government operations is _____ analysis. 8.____
A. cost-benefit
B. budget variance
C. investment capital
D. budget planning program

9. The one of the following assumptions that is LEAST likely to be made by a democratic or permissive type of leader is that 9.____
A. commitment to goals is seldom a result of monetary rewards alone
B. people can learn not only to accept, but also to seek, responsibility
C. the average person prefers security over advancement
D. creativity may be found in most segments of the population

10. In attempting to motivate subordinates, a manager should PRINCIPALLY be aware of the fact that 10.____
A. the psychological qualities of people, in general, are easily predictable
B. fear, as a traditional form of motivation, has lost much of its former power to motivate people in our modern industrial society
C. fear is still the most potent force in motivating the behavior of subordinates in the public service
D. the worker has very little control over the quality and quantity of his output

11. Assume that the following figures represent the number of work-unit that were produced during a week by each of sixteen employees in a division: 11.____

12	16	13	18
21	12	16	13
16	13	17	21
13	15	18	20

If all of the employees of the division who produced thirteen work-units during the week had instead produced fifteen work-units during that same week, then for that week the
   A. mean, median, and mode would all change
   B. mean and mode would change, but the median would remain the same
   C. mode and median would change, but the mean would remain the same
   D. mode, mean, and median would all still remain unchanged in value

12. An important law in motivation theory is called the *law of effect.* This law says that behavior which satisfies a person's needs tends to be repeated; behavior which does not satisfy a person's needs tends to be eliminated. 12.____
The one of the following which is the BEST interpretation of this law is that
   A. productivity depends on personality traits
   B. diversity of goals leads to instability and motivation
   C. the greater the satisfaction, the more likely it is that the behavior will be reinforced
   D. extrinsic satisfaction is more important than intrinsic reward

13. Of the following, the MOST acceptable reason an administrator can give for taking advice from other employees in the organization only when he asks for it is that he wants to 13.____
   A. encourage creativity and high morale
   B. keep dysfunctional pressures and inconsistent recommendations to a minimum
   C. show his superiors and peers who is in charge
   D. show his subordinates who is in charge

14. A complete picture of the communication channels in an organization can BEST be revealed by 14.____
   A. observing the planned paperwork system
   B. recording the highly intermittent patterns of communication
   C. plotting the entire flow of information over a period of time
   D. monitoring the *grapevine*

Questions 15-16.

DIRECTIONS: Questions 15 and 16 are to be answered SOLELY on the basis of the following passage.

Management by objectives (MBO) may be defined as the process by which the superior and the subordinate managers of an organization jointly define its common goals, define each individual's major areas of responsibility in terms of the results expected of him and use these measures as guides for operating the unit and assessing the contribution of each of its members.

The MBO approach requires that after organizational goals are established and communicated, targets must be set for each individual position which are congruent with organizational goals. Periodic performance reviews and a final review using the objectives set as criteria are also basic to this approach.

Recent studies have shown that MBO programs are influenced by attitudes and perceptions of the boss, the company, the reward-punishment system, and the program itself. In addition, the manner in which the MBO program is carried out can influence the success of the program. A study done in the late sixties indicates that the best results are obtained when the manager sets goals which deal with significant problem areas in the organizational unit, or with the subordinate's personal deficiencies. These goals must be clear with regard to what is expected of the subordinate. The frequency of feedback is also important in the success of a management-by-objectives program. Generally, the greater the amount of feedback, the more successful the MBO program.

15. According to the above passage, the expected output for individual employees should be determined 15.____
    A. after a number of reviews of work performance
    B. after common organizational goals are defined
    C. before common organizational goals are defined
    D. on the basis of an employee's personal qualities

16. According to the above passage, the management-by-objectives approach requires 16.____
    A. less feedback than other types of management programs
    B. little review of on-the-job performance after the initial setting of goals
    C. general conformance between individual goals and organizational goals
    D. the setting of goals which deal with minor problem area in the organization

Questions 17-19.

DIRECTIONS: Questions 17 through 19 are to be answered SOLELY on the basis of the following passage.

During the last decade, a great deal of interest has been generated around the phenomenon of organizational development, or the process of developing human resources through conscious organization effort. Organizational development (OD) stresses improving interpersonal relationships and organizational skills, such as communication, to a much greater degree than individual training ever did.

The kind of training that an organization should emphasize depends upon the present and future structure of the organization. If future organizations are to be unstable, shifting coalitions, then individual skills and abilities, particularly those emphasizing innovativeness, creativity, flexibility, and the latest technological knowledge, are crucial, and individual training is most appropriate.

But if there is to be little change in organizational structure, then the main thrust of training should be group-oriented or organizational development. This approach seems better designed for overcoming hierarchical barriers, for developing a degree of interpersonal relationships which make communication along the chain of command possible, and for retaining a modicum of innovation and/or flexibility.

17. According to the above passage, group-oriented training is MOST useful in 17.____
    A. developing a communications system that will facilitate understanding through the chain of command
    B. highly flexible and mobile organizations
    C. preventing the crossing of hierarchical barriers within an organization
    D. saving energy otherwise wasted on developing methods of dealing with rigid hierarchies

18. The one of the following conclusions which can be drawn MOST appropriately from the above passage is that 18.____
    A. behavioral research supports the use of organizational development training method rather than individualized training
    B. it is easier to provide individualized training in specific skills than to set up sensitivity training programs
    C. organizational development eliminates innovative or flexible activity
    D. the nature of an organization greatly influences which training methods will be most effective

19. According to the above passage, the one of the following which is LEAST important for large-scale organizations geared to rapid and abrupt change is 19.____
    A. current technological information
    B. development of a high degree of interpersonal relationships
    C. development of individual skills and abilities
    D. emphasis on creativity

Questions 20-25.

DIRECTIONS: Each of Questions 20 through 25 consist of a statement which contains one word that is incorrectly used because it is not in keeping with the meaning that the quotation is evidently intended to convey. Determine which word is INCORRECTLY used. Select from the choices lettered A, B, C, and D the word which, when substituted for the incorrectly used word, would BEST help to convey the meaning of the statement.

20. One of the considerations likely to affect the currency of classification, particularly in professional and managerial occupations, is the impact of the incumbent's capacities on the job. Some work is highly susceptible to change as the result of the special talents or interests of the classifier. Organization should never be so rigid as not to capitalize on the innovative or unusual proclivities of its key employees. While a machine operator may not be able, even subtly, to change the character or level of his job, the design engineer, the attorney, or the organization and methods analyst might readily do so. Reliance on his judgment and the scope of his assignments may both grow as the result of his skill, insight, and capacity. 20.____
A. unlikely B. incumbent C. directly D. scope

21. The supply of services by the state is not governed by market price. The aim is to supply such services to all who need them and to treat all consumers equally. This objective especially compels the civil servant to maintain a role f strict impartiality, based on the principle of equality of individual citizens vis-à-vis their government. However, there is a clear difference between being neutral and impartial. If the requirement is construed to mean that all civil servants should be political eunuchs, devoid of the drive and motivation essential to dynamic administration, then the concept of impartiality is being seriously utilized. Modern governments should not be stopped from demanding that their hirelings have not only the technical but the emotional qualifications necessary for whole-hearted effort. 21.____
A. determined B. rule C. stable D. misapplied

22. The manager was barely listening. Recently, at the divisional level, several new fronts of troubles had erupted, including a requirement to increase production yet hold down operating costs and somehow raise quality standards. Though the three objectives were basically obsolete, top departmental management was insisting on the simultaneous attainment of them, an insistence not helping the manager's ulcer, an old enemy within. Thus, the manager could not find time for interest in individuals—only in statistics which regiment of individuals, like unconsidered Army privates, added up to. 22.____
A. quantity B. battalion C. incompatible D. quiet

23. When a large volume of data flows directly between operators and first-line supervisors, senior executives tend to be out of the mainstream of work. Summary reports can increase their remoteness. An executive needs to know the volume, quality, and cost of completed work, and exceptional problems. In addition, he may desire information on key operating conditions. Summary reports on these matters are, therefore, essential features of a communications network and make delegation without loss of control possible. 23.____
A. unimportant B. quantity C. offset D. incomplete

24. Of major significance in management is harmony between the overall objectives of the organization and the managerial objectives within that organization. In addition, harmony among goals of managers is impossible; they should not be at cross-purposes. Each manager's goal should supplement and assist the goals of his colleagues. Likewise, the objectives of individuals or non-management members should be harmonized with those of the manager. When this is accomplished, genuine teamwork is the result, and human relations are aided materially. The integration of managers' and individuals' goals aids in achieving greater work satisfaction at all levels. 24.____
   A. competition B. dominate C. incremental D. vital

25. Change constantly challenges the manager. Some of this change is evolutionary, some revolutionary, some recognizable, some non-recognizable. Both forces within an enterprise and forces outside the enterprise cause managers to act and react in initiating changes in their immediate working environment. Change invalidates existing operations. Goals are not being accomplished in the best manner, problems develop, and frequently because of the lack of time, only patched-up solutions are followed. The result is that the mode of management is profound in nature and temporary in effectiveness. A complete overhaul of managerial operations should take place. It appears quite likely that we are just beginning to see the real effects of change in our society; the pace probably will accelerate in ways that few really understand or know how to handle. 25.____
   A. confirms B. decline C. instituting D. superficial

KEY (CORRECT ANSWERS)

1.	C	11.	B
2.	A	12.	C
3.	B	13.	B
4.	B	14.	C
5.	C	15.	B
6.	C	16.	C
7.	C	17.	A
8.	A	18.	D
9.	C	19.	B
10.	B	20.	B

21.	D
22.	C
23.	C
24.	D
25.	D

READING COMPREHENSION
UNDERSTANDING AND INTERPRETING WRITTEN MATERIAL

EXAMINATION SECTION

TEST 1

DIRECTIONS: Each question or incomplete statement is followed by several suggested answers or completions. Select the one that BEST answers the question or completes the statement. *PRINT THE LETTER OF THE CORRECT ANSWER IN THE SPACE AT THE RIGHT.*

Questions 1-5.

DIRECTIONS: Questions 1 through 5 are to be answered SOLELY on the basis of the following passage.

The most effective control mechanism to prevent gross incompetence on the part of public employees is a good personnel program. The personnel officer in the line departments and the central personnel agency should exert positive leadership to raise levels of performance. Although the key factor is the quality of the personnel recruited, staff members other than personnel officers can make important contributions to efficiency. Administrative analysts, now employed in many agencies, make detailed studies of organization and procedures, with the purpose of eliminating delays, waste, and other inefficiencies. Efficiency is, however, more than a question of good organization and procedures; it is also the product of the attitudes and value of the public employees. Personal motivation can provide the will to be efficient. The best management studies will not result in substantial improvement of the performance of those employees who feel no great urge to wok up to their abilities.

1. The above passage indicates that the KEY factor in preventing gross incompetence of public employees is the 1.____
   A. hiring of administrative analysts to assist personnel people
   B. utilization of effective management studies
   C. overlapping of responsibility
   D. quality of the employees hired

2. According to the above passage, the central personnel agency staff SHOULD 2.____
   A. work more closely with administrative analysts in the line departments than with personnel officers
   B. make a serious effort to avoid jurisdictional conflicts with personnel officers in line departments
   C. contribute to improving the quality of work of public employees
   D. engage in a comprehensive program to change the public's negative image of public employees

3. The above passage indicates that efficiency in an organization can BEST be brought about by 3.____
   A. eliminating ineffective control mechanisms
   B. instituting sound organizational procedures
   C. promoting competent personnel
   D. recruiting people with desire to do good work

4. According to the above passage, the purpose of administrative analysts in a public agency is to 4.____
   A. prevent injustice to the public employee
   B. promote the efficiency of the agency
   C. protect the interests of the public
   D. ensure the observance of procedural due process

5. The above passage implies that a considerable rise in the quality of work of public employees can be brought about by 5.____
   A. encouraging positive employee attitudes toward work
   B. controlling personnel officers who exceed their powers
   C. creating warm personal associations among public employees in an agency
   D. closing loopholes in personnel organization and procedures

Questions 6-8.

DIRECTIONS: Questions 6 through 8 are to be answered SOLELY on the basis of the following passage.

<u>EMPLOYEE NEEDS</u>

The greatest waste in industry and in government may be that of human resources. This waste usually derives not from employees' unwillingness or inability, but from management's ineptness to meet the maintenance and motivational needs of employees. Maintenance needs refer to such needs as providing employees with safe places to work, written work rules, job security, adequate salary, employer-sponsored social activities, and with knowledge of their role in the overall framework of the organization. However, of greatest significance to employees are the motivational needs of job growth, achievement, responsibility, and recognition.

Although employee dissatisfaction may stem from either poor maintenance or poor motivation factors, the outward manifestation of the dissatisfaction may be very much like, i.e., negativism, complaints, deterioration of performance, and so forth. The improvement in the lighting of an employee's work area or raising his level of ay won't do much good if the source of the dissatisfaction is the absence of a meaningful assignment. By the same token, if an employee is dissatisfied with what he considers inequitable pay, the introduction of additional challenge in his work may simply make matters worse.

It is relatively easy for an employee to express frustration by complaining about pay, washroom conditions, fringe benefits, and so forth; but most people cannot easily express resentment in terms of the more abstract concepts concerning job growth, responsibility, and achievement.

It would be wrong to assume that there is no interaction between maintenance and motivational needs of employee. For example, conditions of high motivation often overshadow poor maintenance conditions. If an organization is in a period of strong growth and expansion, opportunities for job growth, responsibility, recognition, and achievement are usually abundant, but the rapid growth may have outrun the upkeep of maintenance factors. In this situation, motivation may be high, but only if employees recognize the poor maintenance conditions as unavoidable and temporary. The subordination of maintenance factors cannot go on indefinitely, even with the highest motivation.

Both maintenance and motivation factors influence the behavior of all employees, but employees are not identical and, furthermore, the needs of any individual do not remain orientation toward maintenance factors and those with greater sensitivity toward motivation factors.

A highly maintenance-oriented individual, preoccupied with the factors peripheral to his job rather than the job itself, is more concerned with comfort than challenge. He does not get deeply involved with his work but does with the condition of his work area, toilet facilities, and his time for going to lunch. By contrast, a strongly motivation-oriented employee is usually relatively indifferent to his surroundings and is caught up in the pursuit of work goals.

Fortunately, there are few people who are either exclusively maintenance-oriented or purely motivation-oriented. The former would be deadwood in an organization, while the latter might trample on those around him in his pursuit to achieve his goals.

6. With respect to employee motivational and maintenance needs, the management policies of an organization which is growing rapidly will probably result 6.____
   A. more in meeting motivational needs rather than maintenance needs
   B. more in meeting maintenance needs rather than motivational needs
   C. in meeting both of these needs equally
   D. in increased effort to define the motivational and maintenance needs of its employees

7. In accordance with the above passage, which of the following CANNOT be considered as an example of an employee maintenance need for railroad clerks? 7.____
   A. Providing more relief periods
   B. Providing fair salary increases at periodic intervals
   C. Increasing job responsibilities
   D. Increasing health insurance benefits

8. Most employees in an organization may be categorized as being interested in 8.____
   A. maintenance needs only
   B. motivational needs only
   C. both motivational and maintenance needs
   D. money only, to the exclusion of all other needs

Questions 9-11.

DIRECTIONS: Questions 9 through 11 are to be answered SOLELY on the basis of the following passage.

GOOD EMPLOYEE PRACTICES

As a city employee, you will be expected to take an interest in you work and perform the duties of your job to the best of your ability and in a spirit of cooperation. Nothing shows an interest in your work more than coming to work on time, not only at the start of the day but also when returning from lunch. If it is necessary for you to keep a personal appointment at lunch hour which might cause a delay in getting back to work on time, you should explain the situation to your supervisor and get his approval to come back a little late before you leave for lunch.

You should do everything that is asked of you willingly and consider important even the small jobs that your supervisor gives you. Although these jobs may seem unimportant, if you forget to do them or if you don't do them right, trouble may develop later.

Getting along well with your fellow workers will add much to the enjoyment of your work. You should respect your fellow workers and try to see their side when a disagreement arises. The better you get along with your fellow workers and your supervisor, the better you will like your job and the better you will be able to do it.

9. According to the above passage, in your job as a city employee, you are expected to 9.____
   A. show a willingness to cooperate on the job
   B. get your supervisor's approval before keeping any personal appointments at lunch hour
   C. avoid doing small jobs that seem unimportant
   D. do the easier jobs at the start of the day and the more difficult ones later on

10. According to the above passage, getting to work on time shows that you 10.____
   A. need the job
   B. have an interest in your work
   C. get along well with your fellow workers
   D. like your supervisor

11. According to the above passage, the one of the following statements that is NOT true is: 11.____
   A. If you do a small job wrong, trouble may develop
   B. You should respect your fellow workers
   C. If you disagree with a fellow worker, you should try to see his side of the story
   D. The less you get along with your supervisor, the better you will be able to do your job

Questions 12-15.

DIRECTIONS: Questions 12 through 15 are to be answered SOLELY on the basis of the following passage.

EMPLOYEE SUGGESTIONS

To increase the effectiveness of the city government, the city asks its employees to offer suggestions when they feel an improvement could be made in some government operation. The Employees' Suggestions Program was started to encourage city employees to do this. Through this Program, which is only for city employees, cash awards may be given to those whose suggestions are submitted and approved. Suggestions are looked for not only from supervisors but from all city employees as any city employee may get an idea which might be approved and contribute greatly to the solution of some problem of city government.

Therefore, all suggestions for improvement are welcome, whether they be suggestions on how to improve working conditions, or on how to increase the speed with which work is done, or on how to reduce or eliminate such things as waste, time losses, accidents or fire hazards. There are, however, a few types of suggestions for which cash awards cannot be given. An example of this type would be a suggestion to increase salaries or a suggestion to change the regulations about annual leave or about sick leave. The number of suggestions sent in has increased sharply during the past few years. It is hoped that it will keep increasing in the future in order to meet the city's needs for more ideas for improved ways of doing things.

12. According to the above passage, the MAIN reason why the city asks its employees for suggestions about government operations is to 12.____
   A. increase the effectiveness of the city government
   B. show that the Employees' Suggestion Program is working well
   C. show that everybody helps run the city government
   D. have the employee win a prize

13. According to the above passage, the Employees' Suggestion Program can approve awards ONLY for those suggestions that come from 13.____
   A. city employees
   B. city employees who are supervisors
   C. city employees who are not supervisors
   D. experienced employee of the city

14. According to the above passage, a cash award cannot be given through the Employees' Suggestion Program for a suggestion about 14.____
   A. getting work done faster
   B. helping prevent accidents on the job
   C. increasing the amount of annual leave for city employees
   D. reducing the chance of fire where city employees work

15. According to the above passage, the suggestions sent in during the past few years have 15.____
    A. all been approved
    B. generally been well written
    C. been mostly about reducing or eliminating waste
    D. been greater in number than before

Questions 16-18.

DIRECTIONS: Questions 16 through 18 are to be answered SOLELY on the basis of the following passage.

The supervisor will gain the respect of the members of his staff and increase his influence over them by controlling his temper and avoiding criticizing anyone publicly. When a mistake is made, the good supervisor will take it over with the employee quietly and privately. The supervisor will listen to the employee's story, suggest the better way of doing the job, and offer help so the mistake won't happen again. Before closing the discussion, the supervisor should try to find something good to say about other parts of the employee's work. Some praise and appreciation, along with instruction, is more likely to encourage an employee to improve in those areas where he is weakest.

16. A good title that would show the meaning of the above passage would be 16.____
    A. How to Correct Employee Errors
    B. How to Praise Employees
    C. Mistakes are Preventable
    D. The Weak Employee

17. According to the above passage, the work of an employee who has made a mistake is more likely to improve if the supervisor 17.____
    A. avoids criticizing him
    B. gives him a chance to suggest a better way of doing the work
    C. listens to the employee's excuses to see if he is right
    D. praises good work at the same time he corrects the mistake

18. According to the above passage, when a supervisor needs to correct an employee's mistake, it is important that he 18.____
    A. allow some time to go by after the mistake is made
    B. do so when other employee are not present
    C. show his influence with his tone of voice
    D. tell other employee to avoid the same mistake

Questions 19-23.

DIRECTIONS: Questions 19 through 23 are to be answered SOLELY on the basis of the following passage.

In studying the relationships of people to the organizational structure, it is absolutely necessary to identify and recognize the informal organizational structure. These relationships are necessary when coordination of a plan is attempted. They may be with *the boss*, line supervisors, staff personnel, or other representatives of the formal organization's hierarchy, and they may include the *liaison men* who serve as the leaders of the informal organization. An acquaintanceship with the people serving in these roles in the organization, and its formal counterpart, permits a supervisor to recognize sensitive areas in which it is simple to get conflict reaction. Avoidance of such areas, plus conscious efforts to inform other people of his own objectives for various plans, will usually enlist their aid and support. Planning *without* people can lead to disaster because the individuals who must act together to make any plan a success are more important than the plans themselves.

19. Of the following titles, the one that MOST clearly describes the above passage is 19.____
    A. Coordination of a Function
    B. Avoidance of Conflict
    C. Planning With People
    D. Planning Objectives

20. According to the above passage, attempts at coordinating plans may fail unless 20.____
    A. the plan's objectives are clearly set forth
    B. conflict between groups is resolved
    C. the plans themselves are worthwhile
    D. informal relationships are recognized

21. According to the above passage, conflict 21.____
    A. may, in some cases, be desirable to secure results
    B. produces more heat than light
    C. should be avoided at all costs
    D. possibilities can be predicted by a sensitive supervisor

22. The above passage implies that 22.____
    A. informal relationships are more important than formal structure
    B. the weakness of a formal structure depends upon informal relationships
    C. liaison men are the key people to consult when taking formal and informal structures into account
    D. individuals in a group are at least as important as the plans for the group

23. The above passage suggests that 23.____
    A. some planning can be disastrous
    B. certain people in sensitive areas should be avoided
    C. the supervisor should discourage acquaintanceships in the organization
    D. organizational relationships should be consciously limited

Questions 24-25.

DIRECTIONS: Questions 24 and 25 are to be answered SOLELY on the basis of the following passage.

Good personnel relations of an organization depend upon mutual confidence, trust, and good will. The basis of confidence is understanding. Most troubles start with people who do not understand each other. When the organization's intentions or motives are misunderstood, or when reasons for actions, practices, or policies are misconstrued, complete cooperation from individuals is not forthcoming. If management expects full cooperation from employees, it has a responsibility of sharing with them the information which is the foundation of proper understanding, confidence, and trust. Personnel management has long since outgrown the days when it was the vogue to *treat them rough and tell them nothing*. Up-to-date personnel management provides all possible information about the activities, aims, and purposes of the organization. It seems altogether creditable that a desire should exist among employees for such information which the best-intentioned executive might think would not interest them and which the worst-intentioned would think was none of their business.

24. The above passage implies that one of the causes of the difficulty which an organization might have with its personnel relations is that its employees — 24.____
    A. have not expressed interest in the activities, aims, and purposes of the organization
    B. do not believe in the good faith of the organization
    C. have not been able to give full cooperation to the organization
    D. do not recommend improvements in the practices and policies of the organization

25. According to the above passage, in order for an organization to have good personnel relations, it is NOT essential that — 25.____
    A. employees have confidence in the organization
    B. the purposes of the organization be understood by the employees
    C. employees have a desire for information about the organization
    D. information about the organization be communicated to employees

---

KEY (CORRECT ANSWERS)

1.	D	11.	D
2.	C	12.	A
3.	D	13.	A
4.	B	14.	C
5.	A	15.	D
6.	A	16.	A
7.	C	17.	D
8.	C	18.	B
9.	A	19.	C
10.	B	20.	D

21. D
22. D
23. A
24. B
25. C

TEST 2

DIRECTIONS: Each question or incomplete statement is followed by several suggested answers or completions. Select the one that BEST answers the question or completes the statement. *PRINT THE LETTER OF THE CORRECT ANSWER IN THE SPACE AT THE RIGHT.*

Questions 1-8.

DIRECTIONS: Questions 1 through 8 are to be answered SOLELY on the basis of the following passage.

Important figures in education and in public affairs have recommended development of a private organization sponsored in part by various private foundations which would offer installment payment plans to full-time matriculated students in accredited colleges and universities in the United States and Canada. Contracts would be drawn to cover either tuition and fees, or tuition, fees, room and board in college facilities, from one year up to and including six years. A special charge, which would vary with the length of the contract, would be added to the gross repayable amount. This would be in addition to interest at a rate which would vary with the income of the parents. There would be a 3% annual interest charge for families with total income, before income taxes, of $50,000 or less. The rate would increase by 1/10 of 1% for every $1,000 of additional net income in excess of $50,000 up to a maximum of 10% interest. Contracts would carry an insurance provision on the life of the parent or guardian who signs the contract; all contracts must have the signature of a parent or guardian. Payment would be scheduled in equal monthly installments.

1. Which of the following students would be eligible for the payment plan described in the above passage? A 1.____
   A. matriculated student taking six semester hours toward a graduate degree
   B. matriculated student taking seventeen semester hours toward an undergraduate degree
   C. graduate matriculated at the University of Mexico taking eighteen semester hours toward a graduate degree
   D. student taking eighteen semester hours in a special pre-matriculation program

2. According to the above passage, the organization described would be sponsored in part by 2.____
   A. private foundations
   B. colleges and universities
   C. persons in the field of education
   D. persons in public life

3. Which of the following expenses could NOT be covered by a contract with the organization described in the above passage? 3.____
   A. Tuition amounting to $20,000 per year
   B. Registration and laboratory fees
   C. Meals at restaurants near the college
   D. Rent for an apartment in a college dormitory

4. The total amount to be paid would include ONLY the 4.____
   A. principal
   B. principal and interest
   C. principal, interest, and special charge
   D. principal, interest, special charge, and fee

5. The contract would carry insurance on the 5.____
   A. life of the student
   B. life of the student's parents
   C. income of the parents of the student
   D. life of the parent who signed the contract

6. The interest rate for an annual loan of $25,000 from the organization described in the above passage for a student whose family's net income was $55,000 should be 6.____
   A. 3% B. 3.5% C. 4% D. 4.5%

7. The interest rate for an annual loan of $35,000 from the organization described in the above passage for a student whose family's net income was $100,000 should be 7.____
   A. 5% B. 8% C. 9% D. 10%

8. John Lee has submitted an application for the installment payment plan described in the above passage. John's mother and father have a store which grossed $500,000 last year, but the income which the family received from the store was $90,000 before taxes. They also had $5,000 income from stock dividends. They paid $10,000 in income taxes. 8.____
   The amount of income upon which the interest should be based is
   A. $85,000 B. $90,000 C. $95,000 D. $105,000

Questions 9-13.

DIRECTIONS: Questions 9 through 13 are to be answered SOLELY on the basis of the following passage.

Since the organization chart is pictorial in nature, there is a tendency for it to be drawn in an artistically balanced and appealing fashion, regardless of the realities of actual organizational structure. In addition to being subject to this distortion, there is the difficulty of communicating in any organization chart the relative importance or the relative size of various component parts of an organizational structure. Furthermore, because of the need for simplicity of design, an organization chart can never indicate the full extent of the interrelationships among the component parts of an organization.

These interrelationships are often just as vital as the specifications which an organization chart endeavors to indicate. Yet, if an organization chart were to be drawn with all the wide variety of criss-crossing communication and cooperation networks existent within a typical organization, the chart would probably be much more confusing than informative. It is also obvious that no organization chart as such can prove or disprove that the organizational structure it represents is effective in realizing the objectives of the organization. At best, an organization chart can only illustrate some of the various factors to be taken into consideration in understanding, devising, or altering organizational arrangements.

9. According to the above passage, an organization chart can be expected to portray the 9.____
   A. structure of the organization along somewhat ideal lines
   B. relative size of the organizational units quite accurately
   C. channels of information distribution within the organization graphically
   D. extent of the obligation of each unit to meet the organizational objectives

10. According to the above passage, those aspects of internal functioning which are NOT shown on an organization chart 10.____
   A. can be considered to have little practical application in the operations of the organization
   B. might well be considered to be as important as the structural relationships which a chart does present
   C. could be the cause of considerable confusion in the operations of an organization which is quite large
   D. would be most likely to provide the information needed to determine the overall effectiveness of an organization

11. In the above passage, the one of the following conditions which is NOT implied as being a defect of an organization chart is that an organization chart may 11.____
   A. present a picture of the organizational structure which is different from the structure that actually exists
   B. fail to indicate the comparative size of various organizational units
   C. be limited in its ability to convey some of the meaningful aspects of organizational relationships
   D. become less useful over a period of time during which the organizational facts which it illustrated have changed

12. The one of the following which is the MOST suitable title for the above passage is 12.____
   A. The Design and Construction of an Organization Chart
   B. The Informal Aspects of an Organization Chart
   C. The Inherent Deficiencies of an Organization Chart
   D. The Utilization of a Typical Organization Chart

13. It can be inferred from the above passage that the function of an organization chart is to 13.____
   A. contribute to the comprehension of the organization form and arrangements
   B. establish the capabilities of the organization to operate effectively
   C. provide a balanced picture of the operations of the organization
   D. eliminate the need for complexity in the organization's structure

Questions 14-16.

DIRECTIONS: Questions 14 through 16 are to be answered SOLELY on the basis of the following passage.

In dealing with visitors to the school office, the school secretary must use initiative, tact, and good judgment. All visitors should be greeted promptly and courteously. The nature of their business should be determined quickly and handled expeditiously. Frequently, the secretary should be able to handle requests, deliveries, or passes herself. Her judgment should determine when a visitor should see members of the staff or the principal. Serious problems or doubtful cases should be referred to a supervisor.

14. In general, visitors should be handled by the 14.____
    A. school secretary
    B. principal
    C. appropriate supervisor
    D. person who is free

15. It is wise to obtain the following information from visitors: 15.____
    A. Name
    B. Nature of business
    C. Address
    D. Problems they have

16. All visitors who wish to see members of the staff should 16.____
    A. be permitted to do so
    B. produce identification
    C. do so for valid reasons only
    D. be processed by a supervisor

Questions 17-19.

DIRECTIONS: Questions 17 through 19 are to be answered SOLELY on the basis of the following passage.

Information regarding payroll status, salary differentials, promotional salary increments, deductions, and pension payments should be given to all members of the staff who have questions regarding these items. On occasion, if the secretary is uncertain regarding the information, the staff member should be referred to the principal or the appropriate agency. No question by a staff member regarding payroll status should be brushed aside as immaterial or irrelevant. The school secretary must always try to handle the question or pass it on to the person who can handle it.

17. If a teacher is dissatisfied with information regarding her salary status, as given by the school secretary, the matter should be 17.____
    A. dropped
    B. passed on to the principal
    C. passed on by the secretary to proper agency or the principal
    D. made a basis for grievance procedures

18. The following is an adequate summary of the above passage: 18.____
    A. The secretary must handle all payroll matters
    B. The secretary must handle all payroll matter or know who can handle them
    C. The secretary or the principal must handle all payroll matters
    D. Payroll matter too difficult to handle must be followed up until they are solved

19. The above passage implies that 19.____
    A. many teachers ask immaterial questions regarding payroll status
    B. few teachers ask irrelevant pension questions
    C. no teachers ask immaterial salary questions
    D. no question regarding salary should be considered irrelevant

Questions 20-22.

DIRECTIONS: Questions 20 through 22 are to be answered SOLELY on the basis of the following passage.

The necessity for good speech on the part of the school secretary cannot be overstated. The school secretary must deal with the general public, the pupils, the members of the staff, and the school supervisors. In every situation which involves the general public, the secretary serves as a representative of the school. In dealing with pupils, the secretary's speech must serve as a model from which students may guide themselves. Slang, colloquialisms, malapropisms, and local dialects must be avoided.

20. The above passage implies that the speech pattern of the secretary must be 20.____
    A. perfect
    B. very good
    C. average
    D. on a level with that of the pupils

21. The last sentence indicates that slang 21.____
    A. is acceptable
    B. occurs in all speech
    C. might be used occasionally
    D. should be shunned

22. The above passage implies that the speech of pupils 22.____
    A. may be influenced
    B. does not change readily
    C. is generally good
    D. is generally poor

Questions 23-25.

DIRECTIONS: Questions 23 through 25 are to be answered SOLELY on the basis of the following passage.

The school secretary who is engaged in the task of filing records and correspondence should follow a general set of rules. Items which are filed should be available to other secretaries or to supervisors quickly and easily by means of the application of a modicum of common sense and good judgment. Items which, by their nature, may be difficult to find should be cross-indexed. Folders and drawers should be neatly and accurately labeled. There should never be a large accumulation of papers which have not been filed.

23. A good general rule to follow in filing is that materials should be 23.____
    A. placed in folders quickly
    B. neatly stored
    C. readily available
    D. cross-indexed

24. Items that are filed should be available to 24.____
    A. the secretary charged with the task of filing
    B. secretaries and supervisors
    C. school personnel
    D. the principal

25. A modicum of common sense means _____ common sense. 25.____
    A. an average amount of
    B. a great deal of
    C. a little
    D. no

KEY (CORRECT ANSWERS)

1.	B	11.	D
2.	A	12.	C
3.	C	13.	A
4.	C	14.	A
5.	D	15.	B
6.	B	16.	C
7.	B	17.	C
8.	C	18.	B
9.	A	19.	D
10.	B	20.	B

21. D
22. A
23. C
24. B
25. C

TEST 3

DIRECTIONS: Each question or incomplete statement is followed by several suggested answers or completions. Select the one that BEST answers the question or completes the statement. *PRINT THE LETTER OF THE CORRECT ANSWER IN THE SPACE AT THE RIGHT.*

Questions 1-4.

DIRECTIONS: Questions 1 through 4 are to be answered SOLELY on the basis of the following passage.

The proposition that administrative activity is essentially the same in all organizations appears to underlie some of the practices in the administration of private higher education. Although the practice is unusual in public education, there are numerous instances of industrial, governmental, or military administrators being assigned to private institutions of higher education and, to a lesser extent, of college and university presidents assuming administrative positions in other types of organizations. To test this theory that administrators are interchangeable, there is a need for systematic observation and classification. The myth that an educational administrator must first have experience in the teaching profession is firmly rooted in a long tradition that has historical prestige. The myth is bound up in the expectations of the public and personnel surrounding the administrator. Since administrative success depends significantly on how well an administrator meets the expectations others have of him, the myth may be more powerful than the special experience in helping the administrator attain organizational and educational objectives. Educational administrators who have risen through the teaching profession have often expressed nostalgia for the life of a teacher or scholar, but there is no evidence that this nostalgia contributes to administrative success.

1. Which of the following statements as completed is MOST consistent with the above passage? 1.____
The greatest number of administrators has moved from
   A. industry and the military to government and universities
   B. government and universities to industry and the military
   C. government, the armed forces, and industry to colleges and universities
   D. colleges and universities to government, the armed forces, and industry

2. Of the following, the MOST reasonable inference from the above passage is that a specific area requiring further research is the 2.____
   A. place of myth in the tradition and history of the educational profession
   B. relative effectiveness of educational administrators from inside and outside the teaching profession
   C. performance of administrators in the administration of public colleges
   D. degree of reality behind the nostalgia for scholarly pursuits often expressed by educational administrators

3. According to the above passage, the value to an educational administrator of experience in the teaching profession 3.____
   A. lies in the first-hand knowledge he has acquired of immediate educational problems
   B. may lie in the belief of his colleagues, subordinates, and the public that such experience is necessary
   C. has been supported by evidence that the experience contributes to administrative success in educational fields
   D. would be greater if the administrator were able to free himself from nostalgia for his former duties

4. Of the following, the MOST suitable title for the above passage is 4.____
   A. Educational Administration, Its Problems
   B. The Experience Needed For Educational Administration
   C. Administration in Higher Education
   D. Evaluating Administrative Experience

Questions 5-6.

DIRECTIONS: Questions 5 and 6 are to be answered SOLELY on the basis of the following passage.

Management by objectives (MBO) may be defined as the process by which the superior and the subordinate managers of an organization jointly define its common goals, define each individual's major areas of responsibility in terms of the results expected of him and use these measure as guides for operating the unit and assessing the contribution of each of its members.

The MBO approach requires that after organizational goals are established and communicated, targets must be set for each individual position which are congruent with organizational goals. Periodic performance reviews and a final review using the objectives set as criteria are also basic to this approach.

Recent studies have shown that MBO programs are influenced by attitudes and perceptions of the boss, the company, the reward-punishment system, and the program itself. In addition, the manner in which the MBO program is carried out can influence the success of the program. A study done in the late sixties indicates that the best results are obtained when the manager sets goals which deal with significant problem areas in the organizational unit, or with the subordinate's personal deficiencies. These goals must be clear with regard to what is expected of the subordinate. The frequency of feedback is also important in the success of a management-by-objectives program. Generally, the greater the amount of feedback, the more successful the MBO program.

5. According to the above passage, the expected output for individual employees should be determined 5.____
   A. after a number of reviews of work performance
   B. after common organizational goals are defined
   C. before common organizational goals are defined
   D. on the basis of an employee's personal qualities

6. According to the above passage, the management-by-objectives approach requires 6.____
   A. less feedback than other types of management programs
   B. little review of on-the-job performance after the initial setting of goals
   C. general conformance between individual goals and organizational goals
   D. the setting of goals which deal with minor problem areas in the organization

Questions 7-10.

DIRECTIONS: Questions 7 through 10 are to be answered SOLELY on the basis of the following passage.

Management, which is the function of executive leadership, has as its principal phases the planning, organizing, and controlling of the activities of subordinate groups in the accomplishment of organizational objectives. Planning specifies the kind and extent of the factors, forces, and effects, and the relationships among them, that will be required for satisfactory accomplishment. The nature of the objectives and their requirements must be known before determinations can be made as to what must be done, how it must be done and why, where actions should take place, who should be responsible, and similar programs pertaining to the formulation of a plan. Organizing, which creates the conditions that must be present before the execution of the plan can be undertaken successfully, cannot be done intelligently without knowledge of the organizational objectives. Control, which has to do with the constraint and regulation of activities entering into the execution of the plan, must be exercised in accordance with the characteristics and requirements of the activities demanded by the plan.

7. The one of the following which is the MOST suitable title for the above passage is 7.____
   A. The Nature of Successful Organization
   B. The Planning of Management Functions
   C. The Importance of Organizational Functions
   D. The Principle Aspects of Management

8. It can be inferred from the above passage that the one of the following functions whose existence is essential to the existence of the other three is the 8.____
   A. regulation of the work needed to carry out a plan
   B. understanding of what the organization intends to accomplish
   C. securing of information of the factors necessary for accomplishment of objectives
   D. establishment of the conditions required for successful action

9. The one of the following which would NOT be included within any of the principal phases of the function of executive leadership as defined in the above passage is 9.____
   A. determination of manpower requirements
   B. procurement of required material
   C. establishment of organizational objectives
   D. scheduling of production

10. The conclusion which can MOST reasonably be drawn from the above passage is that the control phase of managing is most directly concerned with the 10.____
    A. influencing of policy determinations
    B. administering of suggestion systems
    C. acquisition of staff for the organization
    D. implementation of performance standards

Questions 11-12.

DIRECTIONS: Questions 11 and 12 are to be answered SOLELY on the basis of the following passage.

Under an open-and-above-board policy, it is to be expected that some supervisors will gloss over known shortcomings of subordinates rather than face the task of discussing team face-to-face. It is also to be expected that at least some employees whose job performance is below par will reject the supervisor's appraisal as biased and unfair. Be that as it may, these are inescapable aspects of any performance appraisal system in which human beings are involved. The supervisor who shies away from calling a spade a spade, as well as the employee with a chip on his shoulder, will each in his own way eventually be revealed in his true light—to the benefit of the organization as a whole.

11. The BEST of the following interpretations of the above passage is that 11.____
    A. the method of rating employee performance requires immediate revision to improve employee acceptance
    B. substandard performance ratings should be discussed with employees even if satisfactory ratings are not
    C. supervisors run the risk of being called unfair by the subordinates even though their appraisals are accurate
    D. any system of employee performance rating is satisfactory if used properly

12. The BEST of the following interpretations of the above passage is that 12.____
    A. supervisors generally are not open-and-above-board with their subordinates
    B. it is necessary for supervisors to tell employees objectively how they are performing
    C. employees complain when their supervisor does not keep them informed
    D. supervisors are afraid to tell subordinates their weaknesses

Questions 13-15.

DIRECTIONS: Questions 13 through 15 are to be answered SOLELY on the basis of the following passage.

During the last decade, a great deal of interest has been generated around the phenomenon of *organizational development,* or the process of developing human resources through conscious organization effort. Organizational development (OD) stresses improving interpersonal relationships and organizational skills, such as communication, to a much greater degree than individual training ever did. The kind of training that an organization should emphasize depends upon the present and future structure of the organization. If future organizations are to be unstable, shifting coalitions, then individual skills and abilities, particularly those emphasizing innovativeness, creativity, flexibility, and the latest technological knowledge, are crucial and individual training is most appropriate.

But if there is to be little change in organizational structure, then the main thrust of training should be group-oriented or organizational development. This approach seems better designed for overcoming hierarchical barriers, for developing a degree of interpersonal relationships which make communication along the chain of command possible, and for retaining a modicum of innovation and/or flexibility.

13. According to the above passage, group-oriented training is MOST useful in in 13.____
    A. developing a communications system that will facilitate understanding through the chain of command
    B. highly flexible and mobile organizations
    C. preventing the crossing of hierarchical barriers within an organization
    D. saving energy otherwise wasted on developing methods of dealing with rigid hierarchies

14. The one of the following conclusions which can be drawn MOST appropriately from the above passage is that 14.____
    A. behavioral research supports the use of organizational development training methods rather than individualized training
    B. it is easier to provide individualized training in specific skills than to set up sensitivity training programs
    C. organizational development eliminates innovative or flexible activity
    D. the nature of an organization greatly influences which training methods will be most effective

15. According to the above passage, the one of the following which is LEAST important for large-scale organizations geared to rapid and abrupt change is 15.____
    A. current technological information
    B. development of a high degree of interpersonal relationships
    C. development of individual skills and abilities
    D. emphasis on creativity

Questions 16-18.

DIRECTIONS: Questions 16 through 18 are to be answered SOLELY on the basis of the following passage.

The increase in the extent to which each individual is personally responsible to others is most noticeable in a large bureaucracy. No one person *decides* anything; each decision of any importance, is the product of an intricate process of brokerage involving individuals inside and outside the organization who feel some reason to be affected by the decision, or two have special knowledge to contribute to it. The more varied the organization's constituency, the more inside *veto-groups* will need to be taken into account. But even if no outside consultations were involved, sheer size would produce a complex process of decision. For a large organization is a deliberately created system of tensions into which each individual is expected to bring work-ways, viewpoints, and outside relationships markedly different from those of his colleagues. It is the administrator's task to draw from these disparate forces the elements of wise action from day to day, consistent with the purposes of the organization as a whole.

16. The above passage is essentially a description of decision-making as 16.____
    A. an organization process
    B. the key responsibility of the administrator
    C. the one best position among many
    D. a complex of individual decisions

17. Which one of the following statements BEST describes the responsibilities of an administrator? 17.____
    A. He modifies decisions and goals in accordance with pressures from within and outside the organization.
    B. He creates problem-solving mechanisms that rely on the varied interests of his staff and *veto-groups.*
    C. He makes determinations that will lead to attainment of his agency's objectives.
    D. He obtains agreement among varying viewpoints and interests

18. In the context of the operations of a central public personnel agency, a *veto-group* would LEAST likely consist of 18.____
    A. employee organizations
    B. professional personnel societies
    C. using agencies
    D. civil service newspapers

Questions 19-25.

DIRECTIONS: Questions 19 through 25 are to be answered SOLELY on the basis of the following passage, which is an extract from a report prepared for Department X, which outlines the procedure to be followed in the case of transfers of employees.

Every transfer, regardless of the reason therefore, requires completion of the record of transfer, Form DT411. To denote consent to the transfer, DT411 should contain the signatures of the transferee and the personnel officer(s) concerned, except that, in the case of an involuntary transfer, the signatures of the transferee's present and prospective supervisors shall be entered in Boxes 8A and 8B, respectively, since the transferee does not consent. Only a permanent employee may request a transfer; in such cases, the employee's attendance record shall be duly considered with regard to absences, latenesses, and accrued overtime balances. In the case of an inter-district transfer, the employee's attendance record must be included in Section 8A of the transfer request, Form DT410, by the personnel officer of the district from which the transfer is requested. The personnel officer of the district to which the employee requested transfer may refuse to accept accrued overtime balances in excess of ten days.

An employee on probation shall be eligible for transfer. If such employee is involuntarily transferred, he shall be credited for the period of time already served on probation. However, if such transfer is voluntary, the employee shall be required to serve the entire period of his probation in the new position. An employee who has occurred a disability which prevents him from performing his normal duties may be transferred during the period of such disability to other appropriate duties. A disability transfer requires the completion of either DT414 if the disability is job-connected, or Form DT415 if it is not a job-connected disability. In either case, the personnel officer of the district from which the transfer is made signs in Box 6A of the first two copies and the personnel officer of the district to which the transfer is made signs in Box 6B of the last two copies, or, in the case of an intra-district disability transfer, the personnel officer must sign in Box 6A of the first two copies and Box 6B of the last two copies.

19. When a personnel officer consents to an employee's request for transfer from his district, this procedure requires that the personnel officer sign Forms 19.____
   A. DT411
   B. DT410 and DT411
   C. DT411 and either Form DT414 or DT415
   D. DT410 and DT411, and either Form DT414 or DT415

20. With respect to the time record of an employee transferred against his wishes during his probationary period, this procedure requires that 20.____
   A. he serve the entire period of his probation in his present office
   B. he lose his accrued overtime balance
   C. his attendance record be considered with regard to absences and latenesses
   D. he be given credit for the period of time he has already served on probation

21. Assume you are a supervisor and an employee must be transferred into your office against his wishes. 21.____
   According to this procedure, the box you must sign on the record of transfer is
   A. 6A   B. 8A   C. 6B   D. 8B

22. Under this procedure, in the case of a disability transfer, when must Box 6A on Forms DT414 and DT415 be signed by the personnel officer of the district to which the transfer is being made? 22.____
   A. In all cases when either Form DT414 or Form DT415 is used
   B. In all cases when Form DT414 is used and only under certain circumstances when Form DT415 is used
   C. In all cases when Form DT415 is used and only under certain circumstances when Form DT414 is used
   D. Only under certain circumstances when either Form DT414 or Form DT415 is used

23. From the above passage, it may be inferred MOST correctly that the number of copies of Form DT414 is 23.____
    A. no more than 2
    B. at least 3
    C. at least 5
    D. more than the number of copies of Form DT415

24. A change in punctuation and capitalization only which would change one sentence into two and possibly contribute to somewhat greater ease of reading this report extract would be MOST appropriate in the 24.____
    A. 2nd sentence, 1st paragraph
    B. 3rd sentence, 1st paragraph
    C. next to the last sentence, 2nd paragraph
    D. 2nd sentence, 2nd paragraph

25. In the second paragraph, a word that is INCORRECTLY used is 25.____
    A. *shall* in the 1st sentence
    B. *voluntary* in the 3rd sentence
    C. *occurred* in the 4th sentence
    D. *intra-district* in the last sentence

KEY (CORRECT ANSWERS)

1. C
2. B
3. B
4. B
5. B
6. C
7. D
8. B
9. C
10. D
11. C
12. B
13. A
14. D
15. B
16. A
17. C
18. B
19. A
20. D
21. D
22. D
23. B
24. B
25. C

INTERPRETING STATISTICAL DATA GRAPHS, CHARTS, AND TABLES

EXAMINATION SECTION

TEST 1

DIRECTIONS: Each question or incomplete statement is followed by several suggested answers or completions. Select the one that BEST answers the question or completes the statement. *PRINT THE LETTER OF THE CORRECT ANSWER IN THE SPACE AT THE RIGHT.*

Questions 1-5.

DIRECTIONS: Questions 1 through 5 are to be answered SOLELY on the basis of the following chart.

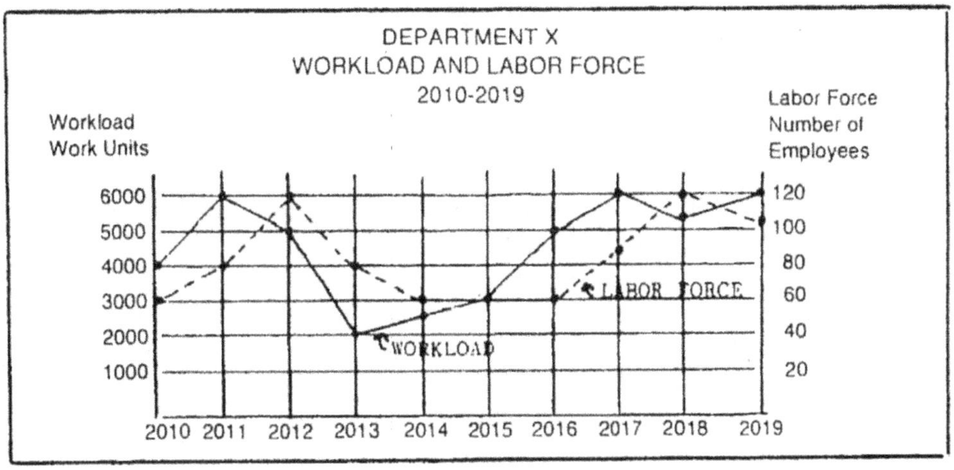

1. The one of the following years for which average employee production was LOWEST was 1.____
   A. 2011 B. 2013 C. 2015 D. 2017

2. The average annual employee production for the ten-year period was, in terms of work units, MOST NEARLY 2.____
   A. 30 B. 50 C. 70 D. 80

3. On the basis of the chart, it can be deduced that personnel needs for the coming year are budgeted on the basis of 3.____
   A. workload for the current year
   B. expected workload for the coming year
   C. no set plan]
   D. average workload over the five years immediately preceding the period

4. The chart indicates that the operation is carefully programmed and that the labor force has been used properly. 4.____
This opinion is
   A. *supported* by the chart; the organization has been able to meet emergency situations requiring more additional work without commensurate increases in staff
   B. *not supported* by the chart; the irregular workload shows a complete absence of planning
   C. *supported* by the chart; the similar shapes of the WORKLOAD and LABOR FORCE curves show that these important factors are closely related
   D. *not supported* by the chart; poor planning with respect to labor requirements is obvious from the chart

5. The chart indicates that the department may be organized in such a way as to require a permanent minimum staff which is too large for the type of operation indicated. 5.____
This opinion is
   A. *supported* by the chart; there is no indication that the operation calls for an irreducible minimum number of employees and application of the most favorable work production records show this to be too high for normal operation
   B. *not supported* by the chart; the absence of any sort of regularity makes it impossible to express any opinion with any degree of certainty
   C. *supported* by the chart; the expected close relationship between workload and labor force is displaced somewhat, a phenomenon which usually occurs as a result of a fixed minimum requirement
   D. *not supported* by the chart; the violent movement of the LABOR FORCE curve makes it evident that no minimum requirements are in effect

KEY (CORRECT ANSWERS)

1. B
2. B
3. A
4. D
5. A

TEST 2

Questions 1-4.

DIRECTIONS: Questions 1 through 4 are to be answered SOLELY on the basis of the chart below, which shows the annual average number of administrative actions completed for the four divisions of a bureau. Assume that the figures remain stable from year to year.

Administrative Actions	DIVISIONS W	X	Y	Z	TOTALS
Telephone Inquiries Answered	8,000	6,800	7,500	4,800	27,100
Interviews Conducted	500	630	550	500	2,180
Applications Processed	15,000	18,000	14,500	9,500	57,000
Letters Typed	2,500	4,400	4,350	3,250	14,500
Reports Completed	200	250	100	50	600
Totals	26,200	30,080	27,000	18,100	101,380

1. In which division is the number of Applications Processed the GREATEST percentage of the total Administrative Actions for that division? 1.____
   A. W B. C. Y D. Z

2. The bureau chief is considering a plan that would consolidate the typing of letters in a separate unit. This unit would be responsible for the typing of letters for all divisions in which the number of letters typed exceeds 15% of the total number of administrative actions. 2.____
   Under this plan, which of the following divisions would CONTINUE to type its own letters?
   A. W and X B. W, X, and Y C. X and Y D. X and Z

3. The setting up of a central information service that would be capable of answering 25% of the whole bureau's telephone inquiries is under consideration. Under such a plan, the divisions would gain for other activities that time previously spent on telephone inquiries. 3.____
   Approximately how much total time would such a service gain for all four divisions if it requires 5 minutes to answer the average telephone inquiry?
   _____ hours,
   A. 500 B. 515 C. 565 D. 585

4. Assume that the rate of production shown in the table can be projected as accurate for the coming year and that monthly output is constant for each type of administrative action within a division. Division Y is scheduled to work exclusively on a four-month long special project during that year. During the period of the project, Division Y's regular workload will be divided evenly among the remaining divisions. 4.____
   Using the figures in the table, what would be MOST NEARLY the percentage increase in the total Administrative Actions completed by Division Z for the year?
   A. 8% B. 16% C. 25% D. 50%

KEY (CORRECT ANSWERS)

1. B
2. A
3. C
4. B

TEST 3

Questions 1-3.

DIRECTIONS: The management study of employee absence due to sickness is an effective tool in planning. Questions 1 through 3 are to be answered SOLELY on the basis of the data below.

Number of Days Absent Per Worker (Sickness)	1	2	3	4	5	6	7	8 OR OVER
Number of Workers	76	23	6	3	1	0	1	0
Total Number of Workers: 400								
Period Covered: Jan. 1 – Dec. 31								

1. The TOTAL number of man days lost due to illness was 1.____
   A. 110 B. 137 C. 144 D. 164

2. What percent of the workers had 4 or more days absence due to sickness? 2.____
   A. .25% B. 2.5% C. 1.25% D. 12.5%

3. Of the 400 workers studied, the number who lost no days due to sickness was 3.____
   A. 190 B. 236 C. 290 D. 346

KEY (CORRECT ANSWERS)

1. D
2. C
3. C

TEST 4

Questions 1-3.

DIRECTIONS: In the graph below, the lines labeled A and B represent the cumulative progress in the work of two file clerks, each of whom was given 500 consecutively numbered applications to file in the proper cabinets over a five-day work week. Questions 1 through 3 are to be answered SOLELY on the basis of the data provided in the graph.

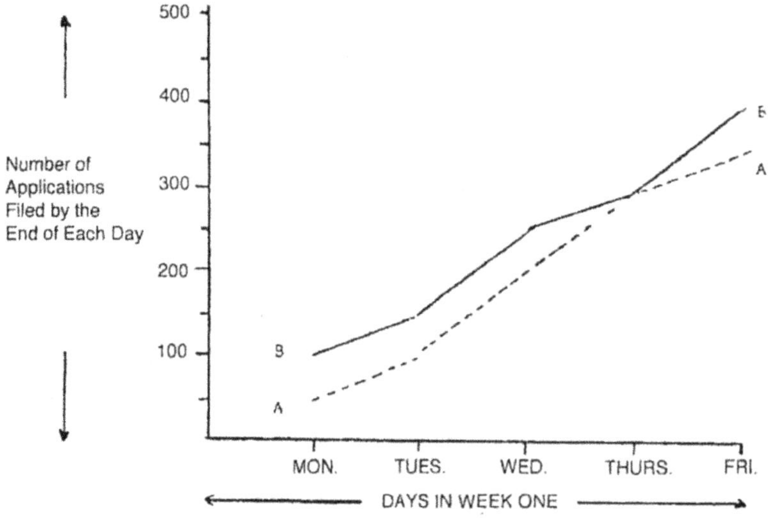

1. The day during which the LARGEST number of applications was filed by both clerks was 1.____
   A. Monday B. Tuesday C. Wednesday D. Friday

2. At the end of the second day, the percentage of applications still to be filed was 2.____
   A. 25% B. 50% C. 66% D. 75%

3. Assuming that the production pattern is the same the following week as the week shown in the chart, the day on which the file clerks will finish this assignment will be 3.____
   A. Monday B. Tuesday C. Wednesday D. Friday

KEY (CORRECT ANSWERS)

1. C
2. D
3. B

TEST 5

Questions 1-3.

DIRECTIONS: Questions 1 through 3 are to be answered SOLELY on the basis of the following information given in the following chart.

Number of Employees Producing Work-Units Within Range in 2009	Number of Work-Units Produced	Number of Employees Producing Work-Units Within Range in 2019
7	500-1000	4
14	1001-1500	11
26	1501-2000	28
22	2001-2500	36
17	2501-3000	39
10	3001-3500	23
4	3501-4000	9

1. Assuming that within each range of work-units produced, the average production was at the mid-point at that range (e.g., category 500-1000 = 750), then the AVERAGE number of work-units produced per employee in 2019 fell into the range 1.____
   A. 1001-1500 B. 1501-2000 C. 2001-2500 D. 2501-3000

2. The ratio of the number of employees producing more than 2000 work-units in 2009 to the number of employees producing more than 2000 work units in 2019 is MOST NEARLY 2.____
   A. 1:2 B. 2:3 C. 3:4 D. 4:5

3. In Department D, which of the following were GREATER in 2019 than in 2009? 3.____
   I. Total number of employees
   II. Total number of work-units produced
   III. Number of employees producing 2000 or fewer work-units
   The CORRECT answer is:
   A. I, II, and III B. I and II, but not III
   C. I and III, but not II D. II and III, but not I

KEY (CORRECT ANSWERS)

1. C
2. A
3. B

TEST 6

Questions 1-9.

DIRECTIONS: Questions 1 through 9 are to be answered SOLELY on the basis of the information contained in the following four charts which relate to a municipal department. These charts show for the fiscal year the total departmental expenditures for salaries for all its employees; the distribution of expenditures for salaries for permanent employees by title; the distribution of all employees, both permanent and temporary by title; and the distribution of temporary employees by title.

For Departmental Expenditures
For Salaries For Fiscal Year.
Total: $129,000,000

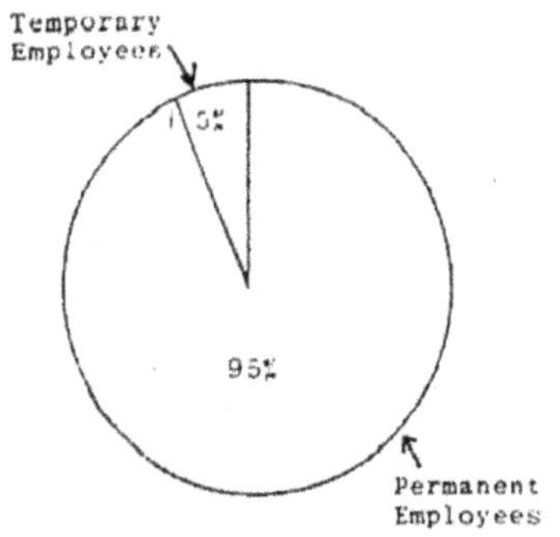

Distribution of Expenditures
For Salaries For Permanent
Employees, By Title.

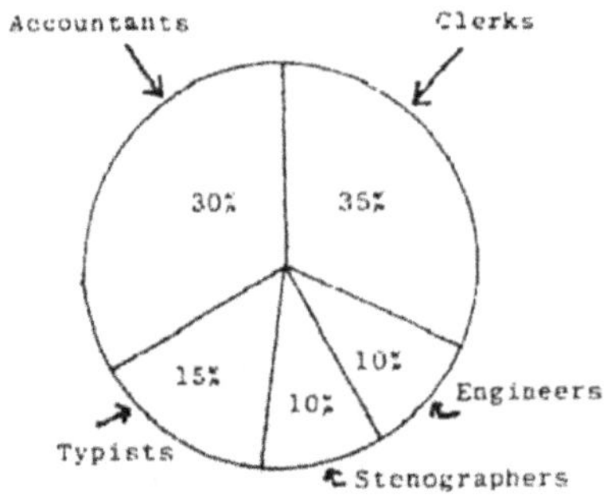

Distribution of All Employees, Both Permanent and Temporary, By Title.
Total Number of Employees: 3,200

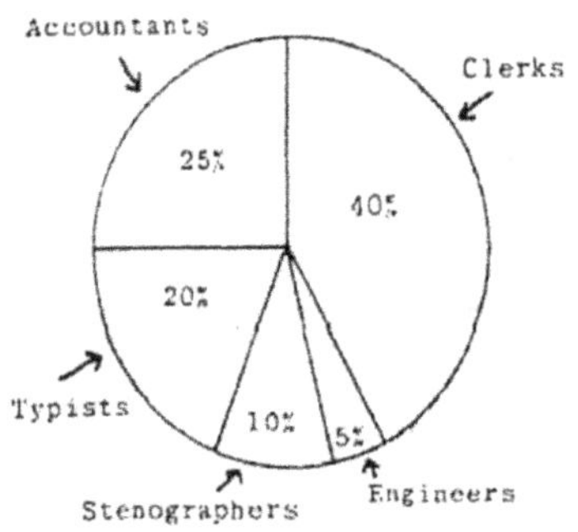

Distribution of Temporary Employees, By Title.
Total Number of Temporary Employees: 150

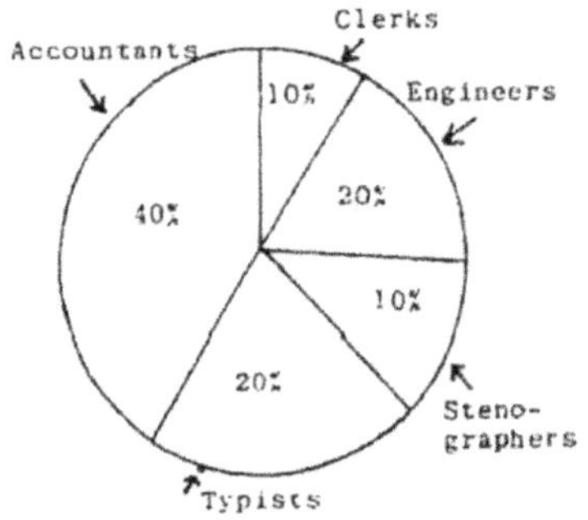

<u>SAMPLE COMPUTATION</u>

The total amount of money expended for the salaries of all the permanent typists can be computed as follows:

By taking 95% of $129,000,000, the total amount of money expended for the salaries of all permanent employees can be obtained. The total amount of money expended for the salaries of all the permanent typists can then be obtained by taking 15% of the money expended for the salaries of all permanent employees.

The answer is $18,382,500.

Candidates may find it useful to arrange their computations on their scratch paper in an orderly manner since the correct computations for one question may also be helpful in answering another question.

1. The TOTAL number of permanent typists is 1.____
   A. 640 B. 670 C. 608 D. 610

2. Of the total departmental expenditures for salaries for both permanent and temporary employees, the percentage allotted to permanent clerks is MOST NEARLY 2.____
   A. 25% B. 31% C. 33% D. 35%

3. The number of permanent employees who are NOT engineers is 3.____
   A. 2,890 B. 3,070 C. 3,040 D. 2,920

4. Assume that the average annual salary of the temporary accountants is $40000. Then, the average annual salary of the permanent accountants exceeds the average annual salary of the temporary accountants by MOST NEARLY 4.____
   A. 25% B. 20% C. 75% D. 40%

5. The average annual salary of the permanent clerks is MOST NEARLY 5.____
   A. $33,300 B. $33,900 C. $35,250 D. $35,700

6. If the temporary stenographers receive 8% of the total salaries allotted to temporary employees, then the average annual salary of the temporary stenographers is MOST NEARLY 6.____
   A. $34,500 B. $38,500 C. $36,000 D. $40,000

7. Assume that the temporary typists receive an average annual salary that is 3% less than the average annual salary that is paid to the permanent typists. Then, the average annual salary of the temporary typists is MOST NEARLY 7.____
   A. $27,850 B. $29,250 C. $30,000 D. $32,150

8. Assume that the average annual salary of the permanent engineers exceeds the average annual salary of the temporary engineers by $30,000. Then, the percentage of the total departmental expenditures for salaries for temporary employees that is allotted to temporary engineers is MOST NEARLY 8.____
   A. 15% B. 20% C. 25% D. 30%

9. If one-half of the permanent accountants earn an average of $45,000 per annum, then the average annual salary of the other permanent accounts is MOST NEARLY 9.____
   A. $51,150 B. $51,750 C. $54,350 D. $57,100

KEY (CORRECT ANSWERS)

1.	D	6.	A
2.	C	7.	B
3.	D	8.	D
4.	A	9.	C
5.	B		

TEST 7

Questions 1-6.

DIRECTIONS: Questions 1 through 6 are to be answered SOLELY on the basis of the information contained in the five charts below.

NUMBER OF UNITS OF WORK PRODUCED IN THE BUREAU PER YEAR

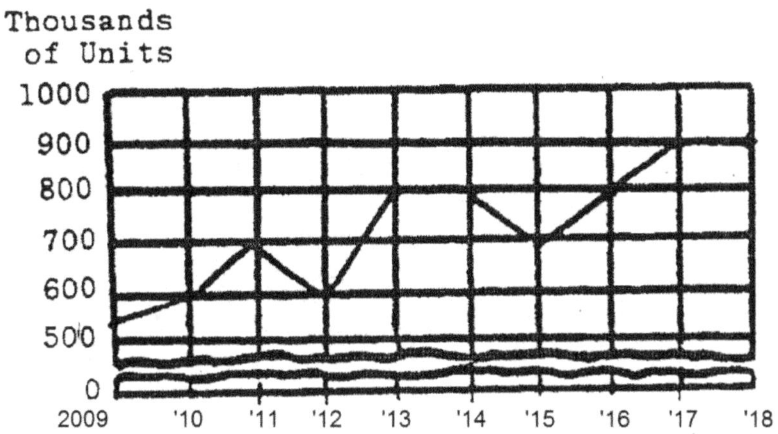

INCREASE IN THE NUMBER OF UNITS OF WORK PRODUCED IN 2018 OVER THE NUMBER PRODUCED IN 2009, BY BOROUGH

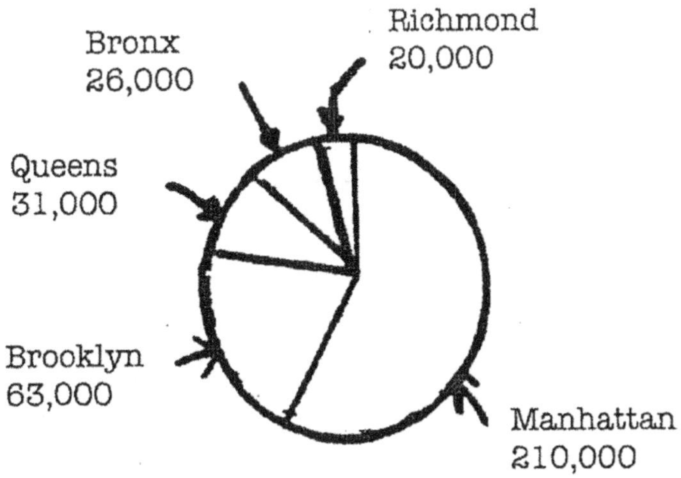

2 (#7)

NUMBER OF MALE AND FEMALE EMPLOYEES PRODUCING THE UNITS OF WORK IN THE BUREAU PER YEAR

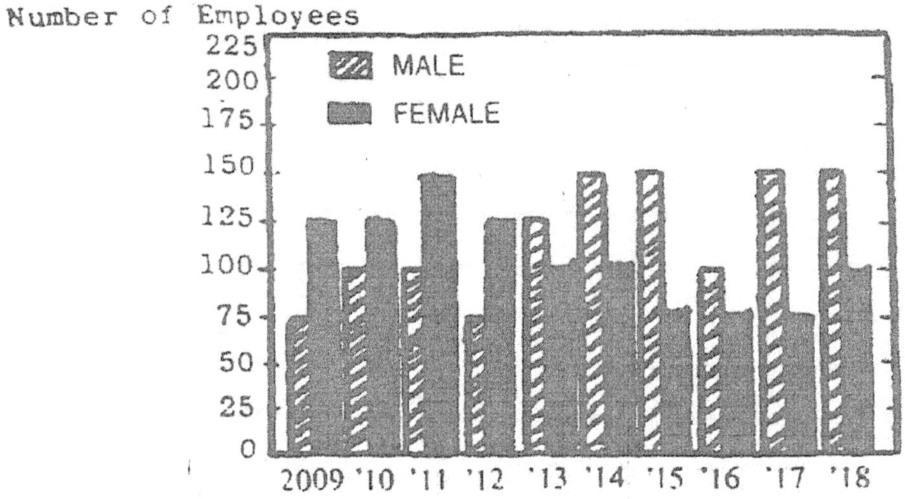

DISTRIBUTION OF THE AGES BY PERCENT OF EMPLOYEES ASSIGNED TO PRODUCE THE UNITS OF WORK IN THE YEARS 2009 AND 2018

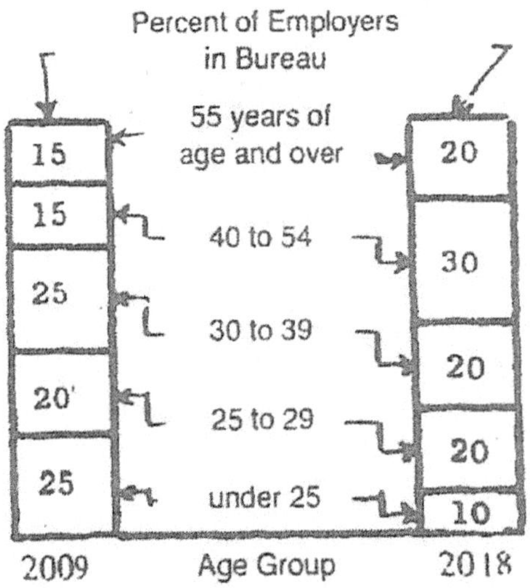

TOTAL SALARIES PAID PER YEAR TO EMPLOYEES ASSIGNED TO PRODUCE THE UNITS OF WORK IN THE BUREAU

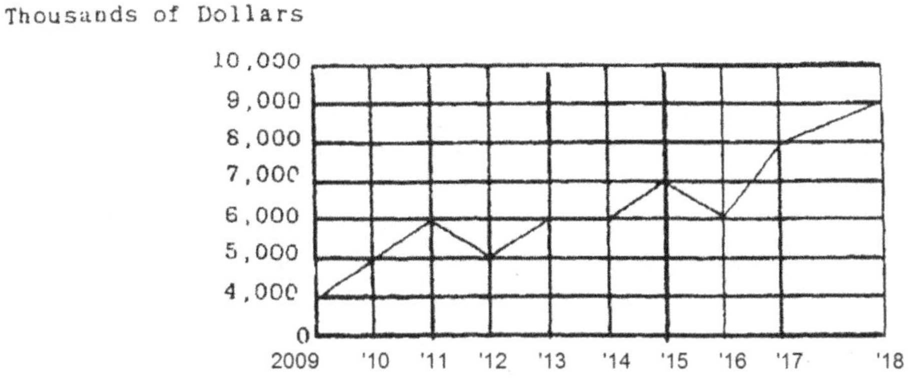

1. The information contained in the charts is sufficient to determine the 1.____
   A. amount of money paid in salaries to employees working in Richmond in 2018
   B. difference between the average annual salary of employees in the Bureau in 2018 and their average annual salary in 2017
   C. number of female employees in the Bureau between 30 and 39 years of age who were employed in 2009
   D. cost, in salary for the average male employee in the Bureau to produce 100 units of work in 2014

2. The one of the following which was GREATER, in the Bureau, in 2014 than it was in 2012 was the 2.____
   A. cost, in salaries, of producing a unit of work
   B. units of work produced annually per employee
   C. proportion of female employees to total number of employees
   D. average annual salary per employee

3. If, in 2018, one-half of the employees in the Bureau 55 years of age and over each earned an annual salary of $42,000, then the average annual salary of all the remaining employees in the Bureau was MOST NEARLY 3.____
   A. $31,750 B. $34,500 C. $35,300 D. $35,800

4. Assume that, in 2009, the offices in Richmond and the Bronx each produced the same number of units of work. Also assume that, in 2009, the offices in Brooklyn, Manhattan, and Queens each produced twice as many units of work as were produced in either of the other two boroughs. 4.____
   Then, the number of units of work produced in Brooklyn in 2008 was MOST NEARLY
   A. 69,000 B. 138,000 C. 201,000 D. 225,000

5. If, in 2016, the average annual salary of the female employees in the Bureau was four-fifths as large as the average annual salary of the male employees, then the average annual salary of the female employees in that year was 5.____
A. $37,500 B. $31,000 C. $30,500 D. $30,000

6. Of the total number of employees in the Bureau who were 30 years of age and over in 2009, _____ must have been _____. 6.____
A. at least 35; females
B. less than 75; males
C. no more than 100; females
D. more than 15; males

KEY (CORRECT ANSWERS)

1. B
2. B
3. C
4. C
5. D
6. A

INTERPRETING STATISTICAL DATA GRAPHS, CHARTS AND TABLES

EXAMINATION SECTION

TEST 1

DIRECTIONS: Each question or incomplete statement is followed by several suggested answers or completions. Select the one that BEST answers the question or completes the statement. *PRINT THE LETTER OF THE CORRECT ANSWER IN THE SPACE AT THE RIGHT.*

Questions 1-8.

DIRECTIONS: Questions 1 through 8 are to be answered SOLELY on the basis of the information and chart given below.

The following chart shows expenses in five selected categories for a one-year period expressed as percentages of these same expenses during the previous year. The chart compares two different offices. In Office T (represented by ▭) a cost reduction program has been tested for the past year. The other office, Office Q (represented by ▨) served as a control, in that no special effort was made to reduce costs during the past year.

RESULTS OF OFFICE COST REDUCTION PROGRAM

Expenses of Test and Control Groups for 2019
Expressed as Percentages of Same Expenses for 2018

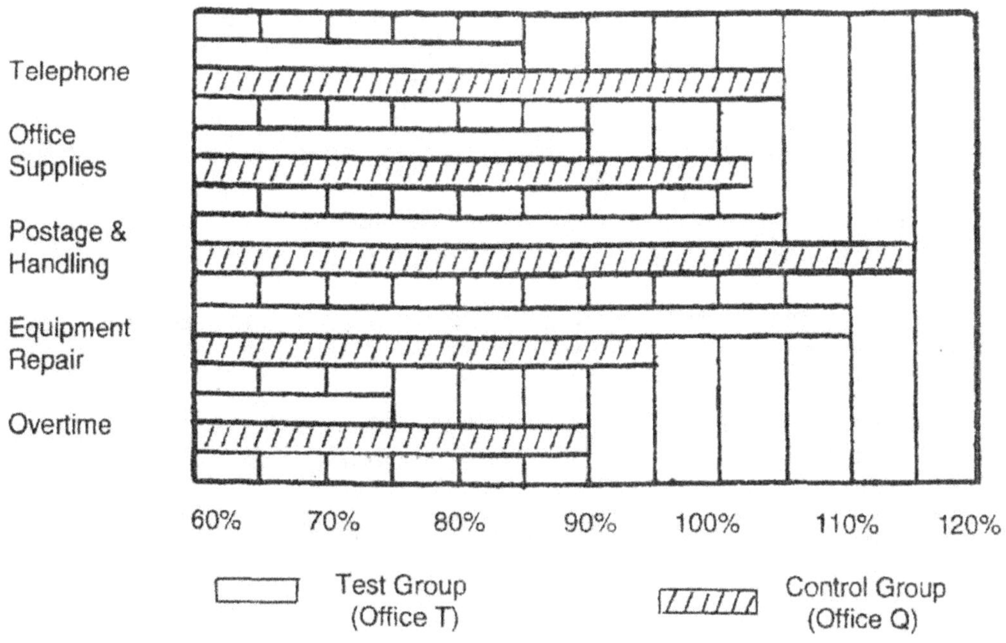

1. In Office T, which category of expenses showed the GREATEST percentage reduction from 2018 to 2019? 1.____
   A. Telephone
   B. Office Supplies
   C. Postage and Mailing
   D. Overtime

2. In which expense category did Office T show the BEST results in percentage terms when compared to Office Q? 2.____
   A. Telephone
   B. Office Supplies
   C. Postage and Mailing
   D. Overtime

3. According to the above chart, the cost reduction program was LEAST effective for the expense category of 3.____
   A. Office Supplies
   B. Postage and Mailing
   C. Equipment Repair
   D. Overtime

4. Office T's telephone costs went down during 2019 by APPROXIMATELY how many percentage points? 4.____
   A. 15
   B. 20
   C. 85
   D. 105

5. Which of the following changes occurred in expenses for Office Supplies in Office Q in the year 2019 as compared with the year 2018? 5.____
   They
   A. *increased* by more than 100%
   B. *remained* the same
   C. *decreased* by a few percentage points
   D. *increased* by a few percentage points

6. For which of the following expense categories do the results in Office T and the results in Office Q differ MOST NEARLY by 10 percentage points? 6.____
   A. Telephone
   B. Postage and Mailing
   C. Equipment Repair
   D. Overtime

7. In which expense category did Office Q's costs show the GREATEST percentage increase in 2019? 7.____
   A. Telephone
   B. Office Supplies
   C. Postage and Mailing
   D. Equipment Repair

8. In Office T, by APPROXIMATELY what percentage did overtime expense change during the past year? 8.____
   It
   A. *increased* by 15%
   B. *increased* by 75%
   C. *decreased* by 10%
   D. *decreased* by 25%

KEY (CORRECT ANSWERS)

1.	D	5.	D
2.	A	6.	B
3.	C	7.	C
4.	A	8.	D

TEST 2

DIRECTIONS: Each question or incomplete statement is followed by several suggested answers or completions. Select the one that BEST answers the question or completes the statement. *PRINT THE LETTER OF THE CORRECT ANSWER IN THE SPACE AT THE RIGHT.*

Questions 1-7.

DIRECTIONS: Questions 1 through 7 are to be answered SOLELY on the basis of the information contained in the following graph which relates to the work of a public agency.

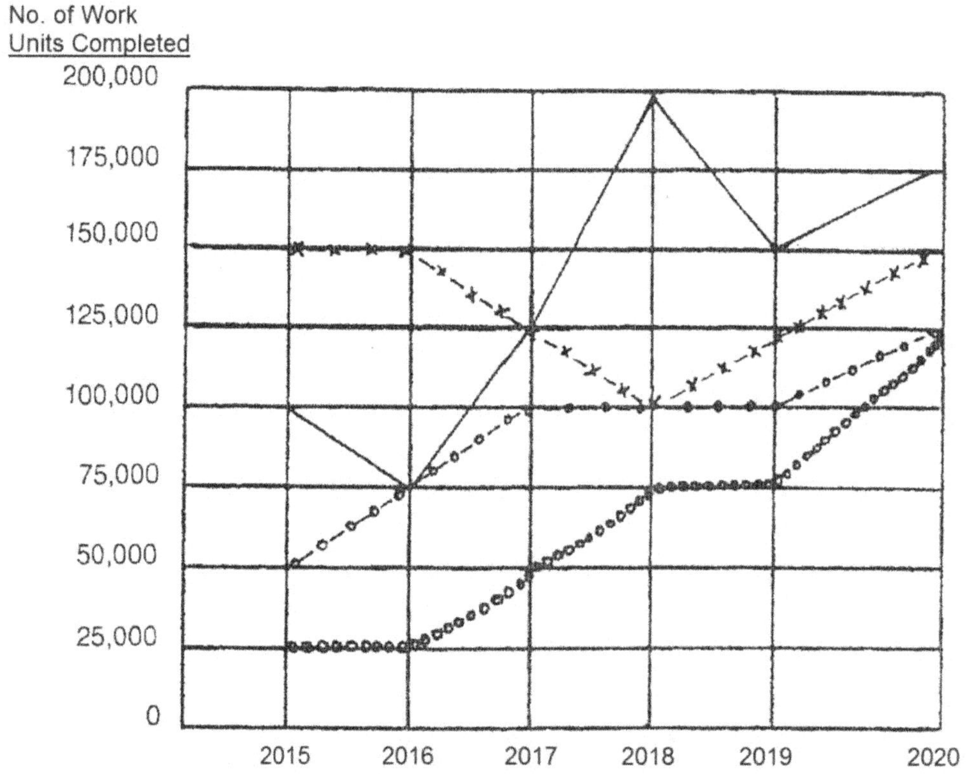

Units of each type of work completed by a public agency from 2015 to 2020.

Letters Written ————— Applications Processed -0-0-0-0-0
Documents Filed –x-x-x-x-x-x-x Inspections Made 0000000000000

1. The year for which the number of units of one type of work completed was less than it was for the previous year while the number of each of the other types of work completed was more than it was for the previous year was 1.____
   A. 2016 B. 2017 C. 2018 D. 2019

2. The number of letters written exceeded the number of applications processed by the same amount in _____ of the years. 2.____
   A. two B. three C. four D. five

3. The year in which the number of each type of work completed was GREATER than in the preceding year was 3.____
   A. 2017 B. 2018 C. 2019 D. 2020

4. The number of applications processed and the number of documents filed were the SAME in 4.____
   A. 2016 B. 2017 C. 2018 D. 2019

5. The TOTAL number of units of work completed by the agency 5.____
   A. increased in each year after 2015
   B. decreased from the prior year in two of the years after 2015
   C. was the same in two successive years from 2015 to 2020
   D. was less in 2015 than in any of the following years

6. For the year in which the number of letters written was twice as high as it was in 2015, the number of documents filed was _____ it was in 2015. 6.____
   A. the same as
   B. two-thirds of what
   C. five-sixths of what
   D. one and one-half times what

7. The variable which was the MOST stable during the period 2015 through 2020 was 7.____
   A. Inspections Made
   B. Letters Written
   C. Documents Filed
   D. Applications Processed

KEY (CORRECT ANSWERS)

1. B
2. B
3. D
4. C
5. C
6. B
7. D

TEST 3

DIRECTIONS: Each question or incomplete statement is followed by several suggested answers or completions. Select the one that BEST answers the question or completes the statement. *PRINT THE LETTER OF THE CORRECT ANSWER IN THE SPACE AT THE RIGHT.*

Questions 1-10.

DIRECTIONS: Questions 1 through 10 are to be answered SOLELY on the basis of the REPORT OF TELEPHONE CALLS table given below.

TABLE – REPORT OF TELEPHONE CALLS

Dept.	No. of Stations	No. of Employees	No. of Incoming Calls In		No. of Long Distance Calls in		No. of Divisions
			2019	2020	2019	2020	
I	11	40	3421	4292	72	54	5
II	36	330	10392	10191	75	78	18
III	53	250	85243	85084	103	98	8
IV	24	60	9675	10123	82	85	6
V	13	30	5208	5492	54	48	6
VI	25	35	7472	8109	86	90	5
VII	37	195	11412	11299	68	72	11
VIII	36	54	8467	8674	59	68	4
IX	163	306	294321	289968	289	321	13
X	40	83	9588	8266	93	89	5
XI	24	68	7867	7433	86	87	13
XII	50	248	10039	10208	101	95	30
XIII	10	230	7550	6941	28	21	10
XVI	25	103	14281	14392	48	40	5
XV	19	230	8475	206	38	43	8
XVI	22	45	4684	5584	39	48	10
XVII	41	58	10102	9677	49	52	6
XVIII	82	106	106242	105889	128	132	10
XIX	6	13	2649	2498	35	29	2
XX	16	30	1395	1468	78	90	2

1. The department which had more than 106,000 incoming calls in 2019 but fewer than 250,000 is 1.____
   A. II B. IX C. XVIII D. III

2. The department which has fewer than 8 divisions and more than 100 but fewer than 300 employees is 2.____
   A. VII B. XIV C. XV D. XVIII

3. The department which had an increase in 2020 over 2019 in the number of both incoming and long distance calls but had an increase in long distance calls of not more than 3 was 3.____
   A. IV B. VI C. XVII D. XVIII

4. The department which had a decrease in the number of incoming calls in 2020 as compared to 2019 and has not less than 6 nor more than 7 divisions is 4.____
   A. IV B. V C. XVII D. III

5. The department which has more than 7 divisions and more than 200 employees but fewer than 19 stations is 5.____
   A. XV B. III C. XX D. XIII

6. The department having more than 10 divisions and fewer than 36 stations, which had an increase in long distance calls in 2020 over 2019, is 6.____
   A. XI B. VII C. XVI D. XVIII

7. The department which in 2020 had at least 7,250 incoming calls and a decrease in long distance calls from 2019 and has more than 50 stations is 7.____
   A. IX B. XII C. XVIII D. III

8. The department which has fewer than 25 stations, fewer than 100 employees, 10 or more divisions, and showed an increase of at least 9 long distance calls in 2020 over 2019 is 8.____
   A. IX B. XVI C. XX D. XIII

9. The department which has more than 50 but fewer than 125 employees and had more than 5,000 incoming calls in 2019 but not more than 10,000, and more than 60 long distance calls in 2020 but not more than 85, and has more than 24 stations is 9.____
   A. VIII B. XIV C. IV D. XI

10. If the number of departments showing an increase in long distance calls in 2020 over 1999 exceeds the number showing a decrease in long distance calls in the same period, select the Roman numeral indicating the department having less than one station for each 10 employees, provided not more than 8 divisions are served by that department. 10.____
    If the number of departments showing an increase in long distance calls in 2020 over 2019 does not exceed the number showing a decrease in long distance calls in the same period, select the Roman numeral indicating the department having the SMALLEST number of incoming calls in 2020.
    A. III B. XIII C. XV D. XX

KEY (CORRECT ANSWERS)

1.	C	6.	A
2.	B	7.	D
3.	A	8.	B
4.	C	9.	A
5.	D	10.	C

TEST 4

DIRECTIONS: Each question or incomplete statement is followed by several suggested answers or completions. Select the one that BEST answers the question or completes the statement. *PRINT THE LETTER OF THE CORRECT ANSWER IN THE SPACE AT THE RIGHT.*

Questions 1-6.

DIRECTIONS: Questions 1 through 6 are to be answered SOLELY on the basis of the information given in the following chart. This chart shows the results of a study made of the tasks performed by a stenographer during one day. Included in the chart are the time at which she started a certain task and, under the particular heading, the amount of time, in minutes, she took to complete the task, and explanations of telephone calls and miscellaneous activities.
NOTE: The time spent at lunch should not be included in any of your calculations.

PAMELA JOB STUDY							
NAME: Pamela Donald							DATE: 9/26
JOB TITLE: Stenographer							
DIVISION: Stenographic Pool							
	TASKS PERFORMED						Explanations of Telephone Calls and Miscellaneous Activities
Time of Start of Task	Taking Dictation	Typing	Filing	Telephone Work	Handling Mail	Misc. Activities	
9:00					22		
9:22						13	Picking up supplies
9:35						15	Cleaning typewriter
9:50	11						
10:01		30					
10:31				8			Call to Agency A
10:39	12						
10:51			10				
11:01				7			Call from Agency B
11:08		30					
11:38	10						
11:48				12			Call from Agency C
12:00	L U N C H						
1:00					28		
1:28	13						
1:41-2:13		32		12			Call to Agency B
X			15				
Y		50					
3:30	10						
3:40			21				
4:01				9			Call from Agency A
4:10	35						
4:45		9					
4:54						6	Cleaning up desk

SAMPLE QUESTION:
The total amount of time spent on miscellaneous activities in the morning is exactly equal to the total amount of time spent
A. filing in the morning
B. handling mail in the afternoon
C. miscellaneous activities in the afternoon
D. handling mail in the morning

Explanation of answer to sample question:
The total amount of time spent on miscellaneous activities in the morning equals 28 minutes (13 minutes for picking up supplies plus 15 minutes for cleaning the typewriter); and since it takes 28 minutes to handle mail in the afternoon, the answer is B.

1. The time labeled Y at which the stenographer started a typing assignment was 1.____
A. 2:15 B. 2:25 C. 2:40 D. 2:50

2. The ratio of time spent on all incoming calls to time spent on all outgoing calls for the day was 2.____
A. 5:7 B. 5:12 C. 7:5 D. 7:12

3. Of the following combinations of tasks, which ones take up exactly 80% of the total time spent on Tasks Performed during the day? 3.____
A. Typing, Filing, Telephone Work, Handling Mail
B. Taking Dictation, Filing, and Miscellaneous Activities
C. Taking Dictation, Typing, Handling Mail, and Miscellaneous Activities
D. Taking Dictation, Typing, Filing, and Telephone Work

4. The total amount of time spent transcribing or typing work is how much MORE than the total amount of time spent in taking dictation? 4.____
A. 55 minutes B. 1 hour
C. 1 hour 10 minutes D. 1 hour 25 minutes

5. The GREATEST number of shifts in activities occurred between the times of 5.____
A. 9:00 A.M. and 10:31 A.M. B. 9:35 A.M. and 11:01 A.M.
C. 10:31 A.M. and 12:00 Noon D. 3:30 P.M. and 5:00 P.M.

6. The total amount of time spent on Taking Dictation in the morning plus the total amount of time spent on Filing in the afternoon is exactly EQUAL to the total amount of time spent on 6.____
A. Typing in the afternoon minus the total amount of time spent on Telephone Work in the afternoon
B. Typing in the morning plus the total amount of time spent on Miscellaneous Activities
C. Dictation in the afternoon plus the total amount of time spent on Filing in the morning
D. Typing in the afternoon minus the total amount of time spent in Handling Mail in the morning

KEY (CORRECT ANSWERS)

1. C
2. C
3. D
4. B
5. C
6. D

TEST 5

DIRECTIONS: Each question or incomplete statement is followed by several suggested answers or completions. Select the one that BEST answers the question or completes the statement. *PRINT THE LETTER OF THE CORRECT ANSWER IN THE SPACE AT THE RIGHT.*

Questions 1-8.

DIRECTIONS: Questions 1 through 8 are to be answered SOLELY on the basis of the information given in the following table.

	Bronx		Brooklyn		Manhattan		Queens		Richmond	
	May	June	May	June	May	June	May	June	May	June
Number of Clerks in Office Assigned To Issue Applications for Licenses	3	4	6	8	6	8	3	5	2	4
Number of Licenses Issued	950	1010	1620	1940	1705	2025	895	1250	685	975
Amount Collected in License Fees	$42,400	$52,100	$77,600	$94,500	$83,700	$98,800	$39,300	$65,500	$30,600	$48,200
Number of Inspectors	4	5	6	7	7	8	4	5	2	4
Number of Inspections Made	420	450	630	710	690	740	400	580	320	440
Number of Violations Found As a Result of Inspections	211	153	352	378	320	385	256	304	105	247

1. Of the following statements, the one which is NOT accurate on the basis of an inspection of the information contained in the table is that, for each office, the increase from May to June in the number of 1.____
   A. inspectors was accompanied by an increase in the number of inspections made
   B. licenses issued was accompanied by an increase in the amount collected in license fees
   C. inspections made was accompanied by an increase in the number of violations found
   D. licenses issued was accompanied by an increase in the number of clerks assigned to issue applications for licenses

2. The TOTAL number of licenses issued by all five offices in the Division in May was 2.____
   A. 4,800 B. 5,855 C. 6,865 D. 7,200

3. The total number of inspectors in all five borough offices in June exceeded the number in May by MOST NEARLY 3.____
   A. 21% B. 26% C. 55% D. 70%

4. In the month of June, the number of violations found per inspection made was the HIGHEST in 4.____
   A. Brooklyn B. Manhattan C. Queens D. Richmond

5. In the month of May, the average number of inspections made by an inspector in the Bronx was the same as the average number of inspections made by an inspector in 5.____
   A. Brooklyn B. Manhattan C. Queens D. Richmond

6. Assume that in June all of the inspectors in the Division spent 7 hours a day making inspections on each of the 21 working days in the month. 6.____
   Then the average amount of time that an inspector in the Manhattan office spent on an inspection that month was MOST NEARLY
   A. 2 hours B. 1 hour and 35 minutes
   C. 1 hour and 3 minutes D. 38 minutes

7. If an average fine of $100 was imposed for a violation found by the Division, what was the TOTAL amount in fines imposed for all the violations found by the Division in May? 7.____
   A. $124,400 B. $133,500 C. $146,700 D. $267,000

8. Assume that the amount collected in license fees by the entire Division in May was 80 percent of the amount collected by the entire Division in April. 8.____
   How much was collected by the entire Division in April?
   A. $218,880 B. $328,320 C. $342,000 D. $410,400

KEY (CORRECT ANSWERS)

1.	C	5.	A
2.	B	6.	B
3.	B	7.	A
4.	D	8.	C

TEST 6

DIRECTIONS: Each question or incomplete statement is followed by several suggested answers or completions. Select the one that BEST answers the question or completes the statement. *PRINT THE LETTER OF THE CORRECT ANSWER IN THE SPACE AT THE RIGHT.*

Questions 1-8.

DIRECTIONS: Questions 1 through 8 are to be answered SOLELY on the basis of the information contained in the chart and table shown below, which relate to Bureau X in a certain public agency. The chart shows the percentage of the bureau's annual expenditures spent on equipment, supplies, and salaries for each of the years 2016-2020. The table shows the bureau's annual expenditures for each of the years 2016-2020.

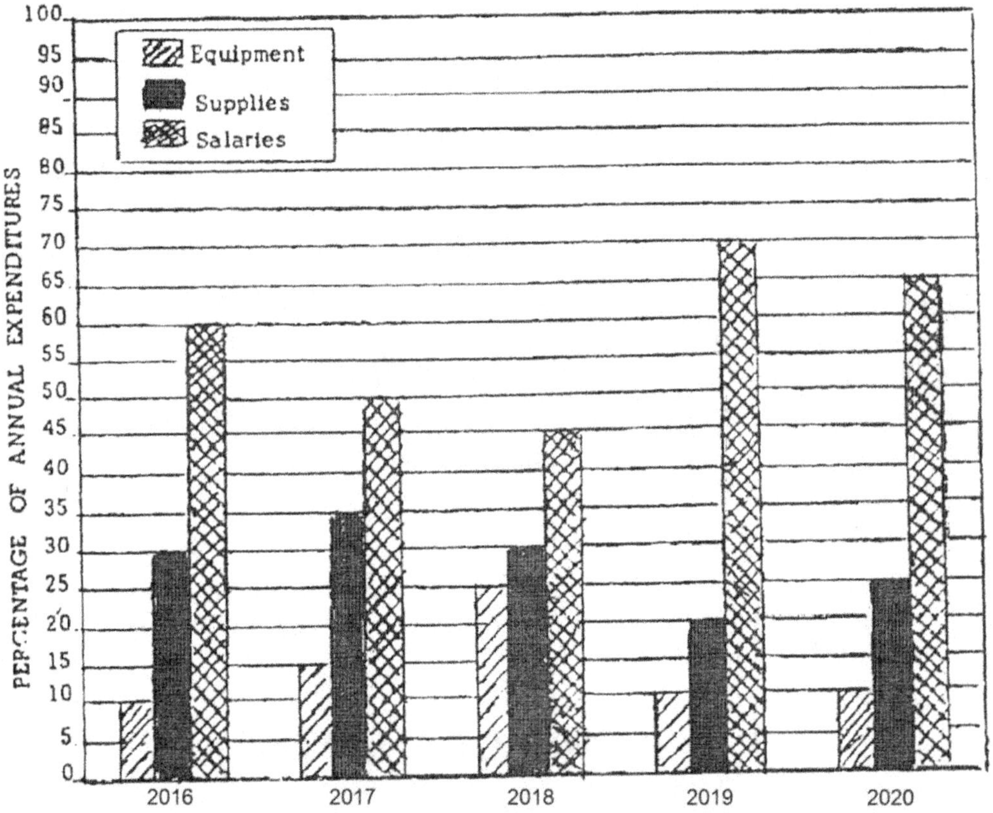

The bureau's annual expenditures for the years 2016-2020 are shown in the following table:

YEAR	EXPENDITURES
2016	$8,000,000
2017	$12,000,000
2018	$15,000,000
2019	$10,000,000
2020	$12,000,000

Equipment, supplies, and salaries were the only three categories for which the bureau spent money.

Candidates may find it useful to arrange their computations on their scratch paper in an orderly manner since the correct computations for one question may also be helpful in answering another question.

1. The information contained in the chart and table is sufficient to determine the 1.____
   A. average annual salary of an employee in the bureau in 2017
   B. decrease in the amount of money spent on supplies in the bureau in 2016 from the amount spent in the preceding year
   C. changes between 2018 and 2019 in the prices of supplies bought by the bureau
   D. increase in the amount of money spent on salaries in the bureau in 2020 over the amount spent in the preceding year

2. If the percentage of expenditures for salaries in one year is added to the percentage of expenditures for equipment in that year, a total of two percentages for that year is obtained. 2.____
   The two years for which this total is the SAME are
   A. 2016 and 2018
   B. 2017 and 2019
   C. 2016 and 2019
   D. 2017 and 2020

3. Of the following, the year in which the bureau spent the GREATEST amount of money on supplies was 3.____
   A. 2020 B. 2018 C. 2016 D. 2016

4. Of the following years, the one in which there was the GREATEST increase over the preceding year in the amount of money spent on salaries is 4.____
   A. 2019 B. 2020 C. 2016 D. 2018

5. Of the bureau's expenditures for equipment in 2020, one-third was used for the purchase of mailroom equipment and the remainder was spent on miscellaneous office equipment. 5.____
   How much did the bureau spend on miscellaneous office equipment in 2020?
   A. $4,000,000 B. $400,000 C. $8,000,000 D. $800,000

6. If there were 120 employees in the bureau in 2019, then the average annual salary paid to the employees in that year was MOST NEARLY 6.____
   A. $43,450 B. $49,600 C. $58,350 D. $80,800

7. In 2018, the bureau had 125 employees. 7.____
   If 20 of the employees earned an average annual salary of $80,000, then the average salary of the other 105 employees was MOST NEARLY
   A. $49,000 B. $64,000 C. $41,000 D. $54,000

8. Assume that the bureau estimated that the amount of money it would spend on supplies in 2021 would be the same as the amount it spent on that category in 2020. Similarly, the bureau estimated that the amount of money it would spend on equipment in 2021 would be the same as the amount it spent on that category in 2020. However, the bureau estimated that in 2021 the amount it would spend on salaries would be 10 percent higher than the amount it spent on that category in 2020. 8.____
The percentage of its annual expenditures that the bureau estimated it would spend on supplies in 2021 is MOST NEARLY
A. 27.5% B. 23.5% C. 22.5% D. 25%

KEY (CORRECT ANSWERS)

1.	D	5.	D
2.	A	6.	C
3.	B	7.	A
4.	C	8.	B

PREPARING WRITTEN MATERIAL

EXAMINATION SECTION

TEST 1

DIRECTIONS: Each short paragraph below is followed by four restatements or summaries of the information contained within it. Select the one that most completely and accurately restates the information given in the paragraph. *PRINT THE LETTER OF THE CORRECT ANSWER IN THE SPACE AT THE RIGHT.*

1. India's night jasmine, or hurshinghar, is different from most flowering plants, in that its flowers are closed during the day, and open after dark. The scientific reason for this is probably that the plant has avoided competing with other flowers for pollinating insects and birds, and relies instead on the service of nocturnal bats that are drawn to the flower's nectar. According to an old Indian legend, however, the flowers sprouted from the funeral ashes of a beautiful young girl who had fallen hopelessly in love with the sun. 1.____
   A. Despite the Indian legend that explains why the hurshinghar's flowers open at dusk, scientists believe it has to do with competition for available pollinators.
   B. The Indian hurshinghar's closure of its flowers during the day is due to a lack of available pollinators.
   C. The hurshinghar of India has evolved an unhealthy dependency on nocturnal bats.
   D. Like most myths, the Indian legend of the hurshinghar's night-flowering has been disproved by science.

2. Charles Lindbergh's trans-Atlantic flight from New York to Paris made him an international hero in 1927, but he lived nearly another fifty years, and by most accounts they weren't terribly happy ones. The two greatest tragedies of his life—the 1932 kidnapping and murder of his oldest son, and an unshakeable reputation as a Nazi sympathizer during World War II—he blamed squarely on the rabid media hounds who stalked his every move. 2.____
   A. Despite the fact that Charles Lindbergh had a hand in the two greatest tragedies of his life, he insisted on blaming the media for his problems.
   B. Charles Lindbergh lived a largely unhappy life after the glory of his 1927 trans-Atlantic flight, and he blamed his unhappiness on media attention
   C. Charles Lindbergh's later life was marked by despair and disillusionment.
   D. Because of the rabid media attention sparked by Charles Lindbergh's 1927 trans-Atlantic flight, he would later consider it the last happy event of his life

3. The United States, one of the world's youngest nations in the early twentieth century, had yet to spread its wings in terms of foreign affairs, preferring to remain isolated and opposed to meddling in the affairs of others. But the fact remained that as a young nation situated on the opposite side of the globe from Europe, Africa, and Asia, the United States had much work to do in 3.____

establishing relations with the rest of the world. So, too, as the European colonial powers continued to battle for influence in North and South America, did the United States come to believe that it was proper for them to keep these nations from encroaching into their sphere of influence.

A. The roots of the Monroe Doctrine can be traced to the foreign policy shift of the United States during the early nineteenth century.
B. In the early nineteenth century, the United States shifted its foreign policy to reflect a growing desire to actively protect its interests in the Western Hemisphere.
C. In the early nineteenth century, the United States was too young and undeveloped to have devised much in the way of foreign policy.
D. The United States adopted a more aggressive foreign policy in the early nineteenth century in order to become a diplomatic player on the world stage.

4. Hertha Ayrton, a nineteenth-century Englishwoman, pursued a career in science during a time when most women were not given the opportunity to go to college. Her series of successes led to her induction into the Institution of Electrical Engineers in 1899, when she was the first woman to receive this professional honor. Her most noted accomplishment was the research and invention of an anti-gas fan that the British War Office used in the trench warfare of World War I. 4.____

A. The British Army's success in World War I can be partly attributed to Hertha Ayrton, a groundbreaking British scientist.
B. Hertha Ayrton was the first woman to be inducted into the Institution of Electrical Engineers.
C. The injustices of nineteenth-century England were no match for the brilliant mind of Hertha Ayrton.
D. Hertha Ayrton defied the restrictions of her society by building a successful scientific career.

5. Scientists studying hyenas in Tanzania's Ngorongoro Crater have observed that hyena clans have evolved a system of territoriality that allows each clan a certain space to hunt within the 100-square-mile area. These territories are not marked by natural boundaries, but by droppings and excretions from the hyenas' scent glands. Usually, the hyenas take these boundary lines very seriously; some hyena clans have been observed abandoning their pursuit of certain prey after the prey has crossed into another territory, even though no members of the neighboring clan are anywhere in sight. 5.____

A. The hyenas of Ngorongoro Crater illustrate that the best way to peacefully co-exist within a limited territory is to strictly delineate and defend territorial borders.
B. While most territorial boundaries are marked using geographical features, the hyenas of Ngorongoro Crater have devised another method.
C. The hyena clans of Ngorongoro Crater, in order to co-exist within a limited hunting territory, have developed a method of marking strict territorial boundaries.
D. As with most species, the hyenas of Ngorongoro Crater have proven the age-old motto: "To the victor go the spoils."

6. The flood control policy of the U.S. Army Corps of Engineers has long been an obvious feature of the American landscape—the Corps seeks to contain the nation's rivers with an enormous network of dams and levees, "channelizing" rivers into small, confined routes that will stay clear of settled flood—plains when rivers rise. As a command of the U.S. Army, the Corps seems to have long seen the nation's rivers as an enemy to be fought; one of the agency's early training films speaks of the Corps' "battle" with its adversary, Mother Nature. 6.____
   A. The dams and levees built by the U.S. Army Corps of Engineers have at least defeated their adversary, Mother Nature.
   B. The flood control policy of the U.S. Army Corps of Engineers has often reflected a military point of view, making the nation's rivers into enemies that must be defeated.
   C. When one realizes that the flood policy of the U.S. Army Corps of Engineers has always relied on a kind of military strategy, it is only possible to view the Corps' efforts as a failure.
   D. By damming and channelizing the nation's rivers, the U.S. Army Corps of Engineers have made America's flood plains safe for farming and development.

7. Frogs with extra legs or missing legs have been showing up with greater frequency over the past decade, and scientists have been baffled by the cause. Some researchers have concluded that pesticide runoff from farms is to blame; others say a common parasite, the trematode, is the culprit. Now, a new study suggests that both these factors in combination have disturbed normal development in many frogs, leading to the abnormalities. 7.____
   A. Despite several studies, scientists still have no idea what is causing the widespread incidence of deformities among aquatic frogs.
   B. In the debate over what is causing the increase in frog deformities, environmentalists tend to blame pesticide runoff, while others blame a common parasite, the trematode.
   C. A recent study suggests that both pesticide runoff and natural parasites have contributed to the increasing rate of deformities in frogs.
   D. Because of their aquatic habitat, frogs are among the most susceptible organisms to chemical ad environmental change, and this is illustrated by the increasing rate of physical deformities among frog populations.

8. The builders of the Egyptian pyramids, to insure that each massive structure was built on a completely flat surface, began by cutting a network of criss-crossing channels into the pyramid's mapped-out ground space and partly filling the channels with water. Because the channels were all interconnected, the water was distributed evenly throughout the channel system, and all the workers had to do to level their building surface was cut away any rock above the waterline. 8.____
   A. The modern carpenter's level uses a principle that was actually invented several centuries ago by the builders of the Egyptian pyramids.
   B. The discovery of the ancient Egyptians' sophisticated construction techniques is a quiet argument against the idea that they were built by slaves.

C. The use of water to insure that the pyramids were level mark the Egyptians as one of the most scientifically advanced of the ancient civilizations.
D. The builders of the Egyptian pyramids used a simple but ingenious method for ensuring a level building surface with interconnected channels of water

9. Thunderhead Mountain, a six-hundred-foot-high formation of granite in the Black Hills of South Dakota, is slowly undergoing a transformation that will not be finished for more than a century, when what remains of the mountain will have become the largest sculpture in the world. The statue, begun in 1947 by a Boston Sculptor named Henry Ziolkowski, is still being carved and blasted by his wife and children into the likeness of Crazy Horse, the legendary chief of the Sioux tribe of American natives. The enormity of the sculpture—the planned length of one of the figure's arms is 263 feet—is understandable, given the historical greatness of Crazy Horse. 9.____
A. Only a hero as great as Crazy Horse could warrant a sculpture so large that it will take morae than a century to complete.
B. In 1947, sculptor Henry Ziolkowski began work on what he imagined would be the largest sculpture in the world—even though he knew he would not live to see it completed.
C. The huge Black Hills sculpture of the great Sioux chief Crazy Horse, still being carried out by the family of Henry Ziolkowski, will some day be the largest sculpture in the world.
D. South Dakota's Thunderhead Mountain will soon be the site of the world's largest sculpture, a statue of the Sioux chief Crazy Horse.

10. Because they were some of the first explorers to venture into the western frontier of North America, the French were responsible for the naming of several native tribes. Some of these names were poorly conceived—the worst of which was perhaps Eskimo, the name for the natives of the far North, which translates roughly as "eaters of raw flesh." The name is incorrect; these people have always cooked their fish and game, and they now call themselves the Inuit, a native term that means "the people." 10.____
A. The first to explore much of North America's western frontier were the French, and they usually gave improper or poorly-informed names to the native tribes.
B. The Eskimos of North America have never eaten raw flesh, so it is curious that the French would give them a name that means "eaters of raw flesh."
C. The Inuit have fought for many years to overcome the impression that they eat raw flesh.
D. Like many native tribes, the Inuit were once incorrectly named by French explorers, but they have since corrected the mistake themselves.

11. Of the 30,000 species of spiders worldwide, only a handful are dangerous to human beings, but this doesn't prevent many people from having a powerful fear of all spiders, whether they are venomous or not. The leading scientific theory about arachnophobia, as this fear is known, is that far in our evolutionary past, some species of spider must have presented a serious enough threat to people that the sight of a star-shaped body or an eight-legged walk was coded into our genes as a danger signal. 11.____

   A. Scientists theorize that peoples' widespread fear of spiders can be traced to an ancient spider species that was dangerous enough to trigger this fearful reaction.
   B. The fear known as arachnophobia is triggered by the sight of a star-shaped body or an eight-legged walk.
   C. Because most spiders have a uniquely shaped body that triggers a human fear response, many humans are afflicted with the fear of spiders known as arachnophobia.
   D. Though only a few of the planet's 30,000 spider species are dangerous to people, many people have an unreasonable fear of them.

12. From the 1970s to the 1990s, the percentage of Americans living in the suburbs climbed from 37% to 47%. In the latter part of the 1990s, a movement emerged that questioned the good of such a population shift—or at least, the good of the speed and manner in which this suburban land was being developed. Often, people began to argue, the planning of such growth was flawed, resulting in a phenomenon that has become known as suburban "sprawl," or the growth of suburban orbits around cities at rates faster than infrastructures could support, and in ways that are damaging to the environment 12.____

   A. The term "urban sprawl" was coined in the 1990s, when the movement against unchecked suburban development began to gather momentum.
   B. In the 1980s and 1990s, home builders benefited from a boom in their most favored demographic segment, suburban new home buyers.
   C. Suburban development tends to suffer from poor planning, which can lead to a lower quality of life for residents
   D. The surge in suburban residences in the late twentieth century was criticized by many as "sprawl" that could not be supported by existing resources

13. Medicare, a $200 billion-a-year program, processes 1 billion claims annually, and in the year 2000, the computer system that handles these claims came under criticism. The General Accounting Office branded Medicare's financial management system as outdated and inadequate—one in a series of studies and reports warning that the program is plagued with duplication, overcharges, double billings, and confusion among users. 13.____

   A. The General Accounting Office's 2000 report proves that Medicare is bloated bureaucracy in need of substantial reform.
   B. Medicare's confusing computer network is an example of how the federal government often neglects the programs that mean the most to average American citizens.

C. In the year 2000, the General Accounting Office criticized Medicare's financial accounting network as inefficient and outdated.
D. Because it has to handle so many claims each year, Medicare's financial accounting system often produces redundancies and errors.

14. The earliest known writing materials were thin clay tablets, used in Mesopotamia more than 5,000 years ago. Although the tablets were cheap and easy to produce, they had two major disadvantages: they were difficult to store, and once the clay had dried and hardened, a person could not write on them. The ancient Egyptians later discovered a better writing material—the thin bark of the papyrus reed, a plant that grew near the mouth of the Nile River, which could be peeled into long strips, woven into a mat-like layer, pounded flat with heavy mallets, and then dried in the sun. 14.____
A. The Egyptians, after centuries of frustration with clay writing tablets, were finally forced to invent a better writing surface.
B. With the bark of the papyrus reed, ancient Egyptians made a writing material that overcame the disadvantages of clay tablets.
C. The Egyptian invention of the papyrus scroll was necessitated in part by a relative lack of available clay.
D. The word "paper" can be traced to the innovations of the Egyptians, who made the first paper-like writing material from the bark of papyrus plant.

15. In 1850, the German pianomaker Heinrich Steinweg and his family stepped off an immigrant ship in New York City, threw themselves into competition with dozens of other established craftsmen, and defeated them all by reinventing the instrument. The company they created commanded the market for nearly the next century and a half, while their competitors—some of the most acclaimed pianomakers in the business—faded into obscurity. And all the while, Steinway & Sons, through their sponsorship and encouragement of the world's most distinguished pianists, helped define the cultural life of the young United States. 15.____
A. The Steinways capitalized on weak competition during the mid-nineteenth century to capture the American piano market.
B. Because of their technical and cultural innovations, the Steinways had an advantage over other American pianomakers.
C. Heinrich Steinweg founded the Steinway piano empire in 1850.
D. From humble immigrant origins, the Steinway family rose to dominate both the pianomaking industry and American musical culture.

16. Feng Shui, the ancient Chinese science of studying the natural environment's effect on a person's well-being, has gained new popularity in the design and decoration of buildings. Although a complex area of study, a basic premise of Feng Shui is that each building creates a unique field of energy which affects the inhabitants of that building or home. In recent years, decorators and realtors have begun to offer services which include a diagnosis of a building's Feng Shui, or energy. 16.____
A. Feng Shui, the Chinese science of balancing environmental energies, has been given more aesthetic quality by recent practitioners.

B. Generally, practitioners of Feng Shui work to create balance within a room, carefully arranging sharp and soft surfaces to create a positive environment that suits the room's primary purpose.
C. The idea behind the Chinese "science" of Feng Sui objects give off certain energies that affect a building's inhabitants has been a difficult one for most Westerners to accept, but it is gaining in popularity.
D. The ancient Chinese science of Feng Shui, which studies the balance of energies in a person's environment, has become popular among those who design and decorate buildings.

17. Because the harsh seasonal variations of the Kansas plains make survival difficult for most plant life, the area is dominated by tall, sturdy grasses. The only tree that has been able to survive and prosper throughout the wide expanse of prairie is the cottonwood, which can take root and grow in the most extreme climatic conditions. Sometimes a storm will shear off a living branch and carry it downstream, where it may snag along a sandbar and take root. 17.____
A. Among the plant life of the Kansas plains, the only tree is the cottonwood.
B. The only prosperous tree on the Kansas plains is the cottonwood, which can take root and grow in a wide range of conditions.
C. Only the cottonwood, whose branches can grow after being broken off and washed down a river, is capable of surviving the climatic extremes of the Kansas plains.
D. Because it is the most widespread and hardiest tree on the Kansas plains, the cottonwood had become a symbol of pioneer grit and fortitude.

18. In the twenty-first century, it's easy to see the automobile as the keystone of American popular culture. Subtract linen dusters, driving goggles, and women's *crepe de chine* veils from our history, and you've taken the Roaring out of the Twenties. Take away the ducktail haircuts, pegged pants, and upturned collars from the teen Car Cult of the Fifties, and the decade isn't nearly as Fabulous. Were the chromed and tailfinned muscle cars of the automobile' Golden Age modeled after us, or were we mimicking them? 18.____
A. Ever since its invention, the automobile has shaped American culture.
B. Many of the familiar names we give historical era, such as "Roaring Twenties" and "Fabulous Fifties," were given because of the predominance of the automobile.
C. Americans' tastes in clothing have been determined primarily by the cars they drive.
D. Teenagers have had a fascination for automobiles ever since the motorcar was first invented.

19. Since the 1960s, an important issue for Canada has been the status of minority French-speaking Canadians, especially in the province of Quebec, whose inhabitants make up 30% of the Canadian population and trace their ancestry back to a Canada that preceded British influence. In response to pressure from Quebec nationalists, the government in 1982 added a Charter of Rights to the constitution, restoring important rights that dated back to the time of aboriginal treaties. Separatism is still a prominent issue, though successive 19.____

referendums and constitutional inquiries have not resulted in any realistic progress toward Quebec's independence.

A. Despite the fact that Quebec's inhabitants have their roots in Canada's original settlers, they have been constantly oppressed by the descendants of those who came later, the British.
B. It seems unavoidable that Quebec's linguistic and cultural differences with the rest of Canada will some day lead to its secession.
C. French-speaking Quebec's activism over the last several decades has led to concessions by the Canadian government, but it seems that Quebec will remain a part of the country for some time.
D. The inhabitants of Quebec are an aboriginal culture that has been exploited by the Canadian government for years, but they are gradually winning back their rights.

20. For years, musicians and scientists have tried to discover what it is about an eighteenth-century Stradivarius violin—which may sell for more than $1 million on today's market—that gives it its unique sound. In 1977, American scientist Joseph Nagyvary discovered that the Stradivarius is made of a spruce wood that came from Venice, where timber was stored beneath the sea, and unlike the dry-seasoned wood from which other violins were made, this spruce contains microscopic holes which add resonance to the violin's sound. Nagyvary also found the varnish used on the Stradivarius to be equally unique, containing tiny mineral crystals that appear to have come from ground-up gemstones, which would filter out high-pitched tones and give the violin a smoother sound. 20.____

A. After carefully studying Stradivarius violins to discover the source of their unique sound, an American scientist discovered two qualities in the construction of them that set them apart from other instruments: the wood from which they were made, and the varnish used to coat the wood.
B. The two qualities that give the Stradivarius violin such a unique sound are the wood, which adds resonance, and the finish, which filters out high-pitched tones.
C. The Stradivarius violin, because of the unique wood and finish used in its construction, is widely regarded as the finest string instrument ever manufactured in the world.
D. A close study of the Stradivarius violin has revealed that the best wood for making violins is Venetian spruce, stored underwater.

21. People who watch the display of fireflies on a clear summer evening are actually witnessing a complex chemical reaction called "bioluminescence," which turns certain organisms into living light bulbs. Organisms that produce this light undergo a reaction in which oxygen combines with a chemical called lucerfin and an enzyme called luciferase. Depending on the organism, the light produced from this reaction can range from the light green of the firefly to the bright red spots of a railroad worm. 21.____

A. Although the function of most displays of bioluminescence is to attract mates, as is the case with fireflies, other species rely on bioluminescence for different purposes.

B. Bioluminescence, a phenomenon produced by several organisms, is the result of a chemical reaction that takes place within the body of the organism.
C. Of all the organisms in the world, only insects are capable of displaying bioluminescence.
D. Despite the fact that some organisms display bioluminescence, these reactions produce almost no heat, which is why the light they create is sometimes referred to as cold light.

22. The first of America's "log cabin" presidents, Andrew Jackson rose from humble backcountry origins to become a U.S. congressman and senator, a renowned military hero, and the seventh president of the United States. Among many Americans, especially those of the western frontier, he was acclaimed as a symbol of the "new" American: self-made, strong through closeness to nature, and endowed with a powerful moral courage. 22.____
    A. Andrew Jackson was the first American president to rise from modest origins.
    B. Because he was born poor, President Andrew Jackson was more popular among Americans of the western frontier.
    C. Andrew Jackson's humble background, along with his outstanding achievements, made him into a symbol of American strength and self-sufficiency.
    D. Andrew Jackson achieved success as a legislator, soldier, and president because he was born humbly and had to work for every honor he ever received.

23. In the past few decades, while much of the world's imagination has focused on the possibilities of outer space, some scientists have been exploring a different frontier—the ocean floor. Although ships have been sailing the oceans for centuries, only recently have scientists developed vehicles strong enough to sustain the pressure of deep-sea exploration and observation. These fiberglass vehicles, called submersibles, are usually just big enough to take two or three people to the deepest parts of the oceans' floors. 23.____
    A. Modern submersible vehicles, thanks to recent technological innovations, are now exploring underwater cliffs, crevices, and mountain ranges that were once unreachable.
    B. While most people tend to fantasize about exploring outer space, they should be turning toward a more accessible realm—the depths of the earth's oceans.
    C. Because of the necessarily small size of submersible vehicles, exploration of the deep ocean is not a widespread activity.
    D. Recent technological developments have helped scientists to turn their attention from deep space to the deep ocean.

24. The panda—a native of the remote mountainous regions of China—subsists almost entirely on the tender shoots of the bamboo plant. This restrictive diet has allowed the panda to evolve an anatomical structure that is completely different from that of other bears, whose paws are aligned for running, stabbing, and scratching. The panda's paw has an over-developed wrist bone that juts out below the other claws like a thumb, and the panda uses this "thumb" to grip bamboo shoots while it strips them of their leaves. 24.____
   A. The panda is the only bear-like animal that feeds on vegetation, and it has a kind of thumb to help it grip bamboo shoots.
   B. The panda's limited diet of bamboo has led it to evolve a thumb-like appendage for grasping bamboo shoots.
   C. The panda's thumb-like appendage is a factor that limits its diet to the shoots of the bamboo plant.
   D. Because bamboo shoots must be held tightly while eaten, the panda's thumb-like appendage ensure that it is the only bear-like animal that eats bamboo.

25. The stability and security of the Balkan region remains a primary concern for Greece in post-Cold War Europe, and Greece's active participation in peacekeeping and humanitarian operations in Georgia, Albania, and Bosnia are substantial examples of this commitment. Due to its geopolitical position, Greece believes it necessary to maintain, at least for now, a more nationalized defense force than other European nations. It is Greece's hope that the new spirit of integration and cooperation will help establish a common European foreign affairs and defense policy that might ease some of these regional tensions, and allow a greater level of Greek participation in NATO's integrated military structure. 25.____
   A. Greece's proximity to the unstable Balkan region has led it to keep a more nationalized military, though it hopes to become more involved in a common European defense force.
   B. The Balkan states present a greater threat to Greece than any other European nation, and Greece has adopted a highly nationalist military force as a result.
   C. Greece, the only Balkan state to belong to NATO, has an isolationist approach to defense, but hopes to achieve greater integration in the organization's combined forces.
   D. Greece's failure to become more militarily integrated with the rest of Europe can be attributed to the failure to establish a common European defense policy.

KEY (CORRECT ANSWERS)

1. A
2. B
3. B
4. D
5. C

6. B
7. C
8. D
9. C
10. D

11. A
12. D
13. C
14. B
15. D

16. D
17. B
18. A
19. C
20. A

21. B
22. C
23. D
24. B
25. A

PREPARING WRITTEN MATERIAL

PARAGRAPH REARRANGEMENT COMMENTARY

The sentences that follow are in scrambled order. You are to rearrange them in proper order and indicate the letter choice containing the correct answer at the space at the right.

Each group of sentences in this section is actually a paragraph presented in scrambled order. Each sentence in the group has a place in that paragraph; no sentence is to be left out. You are to read each group of sentences and decide upon the best order in which to put the sentences so as to form a well-organized paragraph.

The questions in this section measure the ability to solve a problem when all the facts relevant to its solution are not given.

More specifically, certain positions of responsibility and authority require the employee to discover connection between events sometimes, apparently, unrelated. In order to do this, the employee will find it necessary to correctly infer that unspecified events have probably occurred or are likely to occur. This ability becomes especially important when action must be taken on incomplete information.

Accordingly, these questions require competitors to choose among several suggested alternatives, each of which presents a different sequential arrangement of the events. Competitors must choose the MOST logical of the suggested sequences.

In order to do so, they may be required to draw on general knowledge to infer missing concepts or events that are essential to sequencing the given events. Competitors should be careful to infer only what is essential to the sequence. The plausibility of the wrong alternatives will always require the inclusion of unlikely events or of additional chains of events which are NOT essential to sequencing the given events.

It's very important to remember that you are looking for the best of the four possible choices, and that the best choice of all may not even be one of the answers you're given to choose from.

There is no one right way to solve these problems. Many people have found it helpful to first write out the order of the sentences, as they would have arranged them, on their scrap paper before looking at the possible answers. If their optimum answer is there, this can save them some time. If it isn't, this method can still give insight into solving the problem. Others find it most helpful to just go through each of the possible choices, contrasting each as they go along. You should use whatever method feels comfortable and works for you.

While most of these types of questions are not that difficult, we've added a higher percentage of the difficult type, just to give you more practice. Usually there are only one or two questions on this section that contain such subtle distinctions that you're unable to answer confidently. And you then may find yourself stuck deciding between two possible choices, neither of which you're sure about.

PREPARING WRITTEN MATERIAL
PARAGRAPH REARRANGEMENT

EXAMINATION SECTION

TEST 1

DIRECTIONS: The following groups of sentences need to be arranged in an order that makes sense. Select the letter preceding the sequence that represents the best sentence order. *PRINT THE LETTER OF THE CORRECT ANSWER IN THE SPACE AT THE RIGHT.*

1. I. The ostrich egg shell's legendary toughness makes it an excellent substitute for certain types of dishes or dinnerware, and in parts of Africa ostrich shells are cut and decorated for use as containers for water. 1.____
   II. Since prehistoric times, people have used the enormous egg of the ostrich as a part of their diet, a practice which has required much patience and hard work—to hard boil an ostrich egg takes about four hours.
   III. Opening the egg's shell, which is rock hard and nearly an inch thick, requires heavy tools, such as a saw or chisel; from inside, a baby ostrich must use a hornlike projection on its beak as a miniature pick-axe to escape from the egg.
   IV. The offspring of all higher-order animals originate from single egg cells that are carried by mothers, and most of these eggs are relatively small, often microscopic.
   V. The egg of the African ostrich, however, weighs a massive thirty pounds, making it the largest single cell on earth, and a common object of human curiosity and wonder.

   The BEST order is:
   A. V, IV, I, II, III B. I, IV, V, III, II C. IV, II, III, V, I D. IV, V, II, III, I

2. I. Typically only a few feet high on the open sea, individual tsunami have been known to circle the entire globe two or three times if their progress is not interrupted, but are not usually dangerous until they approach the shallow water that surrounds land masses. 2.____
   II. Some of the most terrifying and damaging hazards caused by earthquakes are tsunami, which were once called "tidal waves"—a poorly chosen name, since these waves have nothing to do with tides.
   III. Then a wave, slowed by the sudden drag on the lower part of its moving water column, will pile upon itself, sometimes reaching a height of over 100 feet.
   IV. Tsunami (Japanese for "great harbor wave") are seismic waves that are caused by earthquakes near oceanic trenches, and once triggered, can travel up to 600 miles an hour on the open ocean.
   V. A land-shoaling tsunami is capable of extraordinary destruction; some tsunami have deposited large boats miles inland, washed out two-foot-thick seawalls, and scattered locomotive trains over long distances.

   The BEST order is:
   A. IV, I, III, II, V B. I, III, IV, II, V C. V, I, III, II, IV D. II, IV, I, III, V

3. I. Soon, by the 1940s, jazz was the most popular type of music among American intellectuals and college students. 3.____
   II. In the early days of jazz, it was considered "lowdown" music, or music that was played only in rough, disreputable bars and taverns.
   III. However, jazz didn't take too long to develop from early ragtime melodies into more complex, sophisticated forms, such as Charlie Parker's "bebop" style of jazz.
   IV. After charismatic band leaders such as Duke Ellington and Count Basie brought jazz to a larger audience, and jazz continued to evolve into more complicated forms, white audiences began to accept and even to enjoy the new American art form.
   V. Many white Americans, who then dictated the tastes of society, were wary of music that was played almost exclusively in black clubs in the poorer sections of cities and towns.

   The BEST order is:
   A. V, IV, III, II, I B. II, V, III, IV, I C. IV, V, III, I, II D. I, II, IV, III, V

4. I. Then, hanging in a windless place, the magnetized end of the needle would always point to the south. 4.____
   II. The needle could then be balanced on the rim of a cup, or the edge of a fingernail, but this balancing act was hard to maintain, and the needle often fell off.
   III. Other needles would point to the north, and it was important for any traveler finding his way with a compass to remember which kind of magnetized needle he was carrying.
   IV. To make some of the earliest compasses in recorded history, ancient Chinese "magicians" would rub a needle with a piece of magnetized iron called a lodestone.
   V. A more effective method of keeping the needle free to swing with its magnetic pull was to attach a strand of silk to the center of the needle with a tiny piece of wax.

   The BEST order is:
   A. IV, II, V, I, III B. IV, III, V, II, I C. IV, V, II, I, III D. IV, I, III, V, II

5. I The now-famous first mate of the *H.M.S. Bounty*, Fletcher Christian, founded one of the world's most peculiar civilizations in 1790. 5.____
   II. The men knew they had just committed a crime for which they could be hanged, so they set sail for Pitcairn, a remote, abandoned island in the far eastern region of the Polynesian archipelago, accompanied by twelve Polynesian women and six men.
   III. In a mutiny that has become legendary, Christian and the others forced Captain Bligh into a lifeboat and set him adrift off the coast of Tonga in April of 1789.
   IV. In early 1790, the *Bounty* landed at Pitcairn Island, where the men lived out the rest of their lives and founded an isolated community which to this day includes direct descendants of Christian and the other Crewmen.

V. The *Bounty*, commanded by Captain William Bligh, was in the middle of a global voyage, and Christian and his shipmates had come to the conclusion that Bligh was a reckless madman who would lead them to their deaths unless they took the ship from him.

The BEST order is:

A. IV, V, III, II, I B. I, III, V, II, IV C. I, V, III, II, IV D. III, I, V, IV, II

6. I. But once the vines had been led to make orchids, the flowers had to be carefully hand-pollinated, because unpollinated orchids usually lasted less than a day, wilting and dropping off the vine before it had even become dark. 6.____

II. The Totonac farmers discovered that looping a vine back around once it reached a five-foot height on its host tree would cause the vine to flower.

III. Though they knew how to process the fruit pods and extract vanilla's flavoring agent, the Totonacs also knew that a wild vanilla vine did not produce abundant flowers or fruit.

IV. Wild vines climbed along the trunks and canopies of trees, and this constant upward growth diverted most of the vine's energy to making leaves instead of the orchid flowers that once pollinated, would produce the flavorful pods.

V. Hundreds of years before vanilla became a prized food flavoring in Europe and the Western World, the Totonac Indians of the Mexican Gulf Coast were skilled cultivators of the vanilla vine, whose fruit they literally worshipped as a goddess.

The BEST order is:

A. II, III, IV, I, V B. II, IV, III, I, V C. V, III, IV, II, I D. III, IV, I, II, V

7. I. Once airborne, the spider is at the mercy of the air currents—usually the spider takes a brief journey, traveling close to the ground, but some have been found in air samples collected as high as 10,000 feet, or been reported landing on ships far out at sea. 7.____

II. Once a young spider has hatched, it must leave the environment into which it was born as quickly as possible, in order to avoid competing with its hundreds of brothers and sisters for food.

III. The silk rises into warm air currents, and as soon as the pull feels adequate the spider lets go and drifts up into the air, suspended from the silk strand in the same way that a person might parasail.

IV. To help young spiders do this, many species have adapted a practice known as "aerial dispersal," or, in common speech, "ballooning."

V. A spider that wants to leave its surroundings quickly will climb to the top of a grass system or twig, face into the wind, and aim its back end into the air, releasing a long stream of silk from the glands near the tip of its abdomen.

The BEST order is:

A. V, IV, II, III, I B. V, II, IV, I, III C. II, V, IV, III, I D. II, IV, V, III, I

8. I. For about a year, Tycho worked at a castle in Prague with a scientist named Johannes Kepler, but their association was cut short by another argument that drove Kepler out of the castle, to later develop, on his own, the theory of planetary orbits. 8.____
II. Tycho found life without a nose embarrassing, so he made a new nose for himself out of silver, which reportedly remained glued to his face for the rest of his life.
III. Tycho Brahe, the 17th-century Danish astronomer, is today more famous for his odd and arrogant personality than for any contribution he has made to our knowledge of the stars and planets.
IV. Early in his career, as a student at Rostock University, Tycho got into an argument with another student about who was the better mathematician, and the two became so angry that the argument turned into a sword fight, during which Tycho's nose was sliced off.
V. Later in his life, Tycho's arrogance may have kept him from playing a part in one of the greatest astronomical discoveries in history: the elliptical orbits of the solar system's planets.
The BEST order is:
A. I, IV, II, III, V B. IV, II, III, V, I C. IV, II, I, III, V D. III, IV, II, V, I

9. I. The processionaries are so used to this routine that if a person picks up the end of a silk line and brings it back to the origin—creating a closed circle—the caterpillars may travel around and around for days, sometimes starving or freezing, without changing course. 9.____
II. Rather than relying on sight or sound, the other caterpillars, who are lined up end-to-end behind the leader, travel to and from their nests by walking on this silk line, and each will reinforce it by laying down its own marking line as it passes over.
III. In order to insure the safety of individuals, the processionary caterpillar nests in a tree with dozens of other caterpillars, and at night, when it is safest, they all leave together in search of food.
IV. The processionary caterpillar of the European continent is a perfect illustration of how much some inspect species rely on instinct in their daily routines.
V. As they leave their nests, the processionaries form a single-file line behind a leader who spins and lays out a silk line to mark the chosen path.
The BEST order is:
A. IV, III, V, II, I B. III, V, IV, II, I C. III, V, II, I, IV D. IV, V, III, I, II

10. I. Often, the child is also given a handcrafted walker or push cart, to provide support for its first upright explorations. 10.____
II. In traditional Indian families, a child's first steps are celebrated as a ceremonial event, rooted in ancient myth.
III. These carts are often intricately designed to resemble the chariot of Krishna, an important figure in Indian mythology.
IV. The sound of these anklet bells is intended to mimic the footsteps of the legendary child Rama, who is celebrated in devotional songs throughout India.

V. When the child's parents see that the child is ready to begin walking, they will fit it with specially designed ankle bracelets, adorned with gently ringing bells.

The BEST order is:

A. II, III, IV, I, V B. II, V, III, I, IV C. V, IV, I, III, II D. V, III, II, I, IV

11. I. The settlers planted Osage oranges all across Middle America, and today long lines and rectangles of Osage orange trees can still be seen on the prairies, running along the former boundaries of farms that no longer exist. 11.____

II. After trying sod walls and water-filled ditches with no success, American farmers began to look for a plant that was adaptable to prairie weather, and that could be trimmed into a hedge that was "pig-tight, horse-high, and bull-strong."

III. The tree, so named because it bore a large (but inedible) fruit the size of an orange, was among the sturdiest and hardiest of American trees, and was prized among Native Americans for the strength and flexibility of bows which were made from its wood.

IV. The first people to practice agriculture on the American flatlands were faced with an important problem: what would they use to fence their land in a place that was almost entirely without trees or rocks?

V. Finally, an Illinois farmer brought the settlers a tree that was native to the land between the Red and Arkansas rivers, a tree called the Osage orange.

The BEST order is:

A. II, I, V, III, IV B. I, II, III, IV, V C. IV, II, V, III, I D. IV, II, I, III, V

12. I. After about ten minutes of such spirited and complicated activity, the head dancer is free to make up his or her own movements while maintaining the interest of the New Year's crowd. 12.____

II. The dancer will then perform a series of leg kicks, while at the same time operating the lion's mouth with his own hand and moving the ears and eyes by means of a string which is attached to the dancer's own mouth.

III. The most difficult role of this dance belongs to the one who controls the lion's head; this person must lead all the other "parts" of the lion through the choreographed segments of the dance.

IV. The head dancer begins with a complex series of steps. alternately stepping forward with the head raised, and then retreating a few steps while lowering the head, a movement that is intended to create the impression that the lion is keeping a watchful eye for anything evil.

V. When performing a traditional Chinese New Year's lion dance, several performers must fit themselves inside a large lion costume and work together to enact different parts of the dance.

The BEST order is:

A. V, III, IV, II, I B. III, IV, II, V, I C. III, I, V, IV, II D. IV, II, III, V, I

13. I. For many years the shell of the chambered nautilus was treasured in Europe for its beauty and intricacy, but collectors were unaware that they were in possession of the structure that marked a "missing link" in the evolution of marine mollusks. 13.____
II. The nautilus, however, evolved a series of enclosed chambers in its shell, and invented a new use for the structure: the shell began to serve as a buoyancy device.
III. Equipped with this new flotation device, the nautilus did not need the single, muscular foot of its predecessors, but instead developed flaps, tentacles, and a gentle form of jet propulsion that transformed it into the first mollusk able to take command of its own density and explore a three-dimensional world.
IV. By pumping and adjusting air pressure into the chambers, the nautilus could spend the day resting on the bottom, and then rise toward the surface at night in search of food.
V. The nautilus shell looks like a large snail shell, similar to those of its ancestors, who used their shells as protective coverings while they were anchored to the sea floor.

The BEST order is:

A. V, II, IV, I, III B. V, I, II, III, IV C. I, II, V, III, IV D. I, V, II, IV, III

14. I. While France and England battled for control of the region, the Acadiens prospered on the fertile farmland, which was finally secured by England in 1713. 14.____
II. Early in the 17th century, settlers from Western France founded a colony called Acadie in what is now the Canadian province of Nova Scotia.
III. At this time, English officials feared the presence of spies among the Acadiens who might be loyal to their French homeland, and the Acadiens were deported to spots along the Atlantic and Caribbean shores of America.
IV. The French settlers remained on this land, under English rule, for around forty years, until the beginning of the French and Indian War, another conflict between France and England.
V. As the Acadien refugees drifted toward a final home in Southern Louisiana, neighbors shortened their name to "Cadien," and finally "Cajun," the name which the descendants of early Acadiens still call themselves.

The BEST order is:

A. I, IV, II, III, V B. II, I, III, V, IV C. II, I, IV, III, V D. V, II, III, IV, I

15. I. Traditional households in the Eastern and Western regions of Africa serve two meals a day—one at around noon, and the other in the evening. 15.____
II. The starch is then used in the way that Americans might use a spoon, to scoop up a portion of the main dish on the person's plate.
III. The reason for the starch's inclusion in every meal has to do with taste as well as nutrition; African food can be very spicy, and the starch is known to cool the burning effect of the main dish.
IV. When serving these meals, the main dish is usually served on individual plates, and the starch is served on a communal plate, from which diners break off a piece of bread or scoop rice or fufu in their fingers.

V. The typical meals usually consist of a thick stew or soup as the main course, and an accompanying starch—either bread, rice, or *fufu*, a starchy grain paste similar in consistency to mashed potatoes.

The BEST order is:

A. V, II, III, IV, I B. V, I, IV, III, II C. I, IV, V, III, II D. I, V, IV, II, III

16. I. In the early days of the American Midwest, Indiana settlers sometimes came together to hold an event called an apple peeling, where neighboring settlers gathered at the homestead of a host family to help prepare the hosts' apple crop for cooking, canning, and making apple butter. 16.____

II. At the beginning of the event, each peeler sat down in front of a ten- or twenty-gallon stone jar and was given a crock of apples and a paring knife.

III. Once a peeler had finished with a crock, another was placed next to him; if the peeler was an unmarried man, he kept a strict count of the number of apples he had peeled, because the winner was allowed to kiss the girl of his choice.

IV. The peeling usually ended by 9:30 in the evening, when the neighbors gathered in the host family's parlor for a dance social.

V. The apples were peeled, cored, and quartered, and then placed into the jar.

The BEST order is:

A. I, V, III, IV, II B. II, V, III, IV, I C. I, II, V, III, IV D. II, I, V, IV, III

17. I. If your pet turtle is a land turtle and is native to temperate climates, it will stop eating some time in October, which should be your cue to prepare the turtle for hibernation. 17.____

II. The box should then be covered with a wire screen, which will protect the turtle from any rodents or predators that might want to take advantage of a motionless and helpless animal.

III. When your turtle hasn't eaten for a while and appears ready to hibernate, it should be moved to its winter quarters, most likely a cellar or garage, where the temperature should range between 40° and 45°F.

IV. Instead of feeding the turtle, you should bathe it every day in warm water, to encourage the turtle to empty its intestines in preparation for its long winter sleep.

V. Here the turtle should be placed in a well-ventilated box whose bottom is covered with a moisture-absorbing layer of clay beads, and then filled three-fourths full with almost dry peat moss or wood chips, into which the turtle will burrow and sleep for several months.

The BEST order is:

A. I, IV, III, V, II B. III, IV, II, V, I C. III, II, IV, I, V D. IV, V, II, III, I

18. I. Once he has reached the nest, the hunter uses two sturdy bamboo poles like huge chopsticks to pull the next away from the mountainside, into a large basket that will be lowered to people waiting below. 18.____

II. The world's largest honeybees colonize the Nealese mountainsides, building honeycombs as large as a person on sheer rock faces that are often hundreds of feet high.

III. In the remote mountain country of Nepal, a small band of "honey hunters" carry out a tradition so ancient that 10,000 year-old drawings of the practice have been found in the caves of Nepal.
IV. To harvest the honey and beeswax from these combs, a honey hunter climbs above the nests, lowers a long bamboo-fiber ladder over the cliff, and then climbs down.
V. Throughout this dangerous practice, the hunter is stung repeatedly, and only the veterans, with skin that has been toughened over the years, are able to return from a hunt without the painful swelling caused by stings.

The BEST order is:
A. II, IV, III, V, I B. II, IV, I, V, III C. V, III, II, IV, I D. III, II, IV, I, V

19. I. After the Romans left Britain, there were relentless attacks on the islands from the barbarian tribes of northern Germany—the Angles, Saxons, and Jutes. 19.____
II. As the empire weakened, Roman soldiers withdrew from Britain, leaving behind a country that continued to practice the Christian religion that had been introduced by the Romans.
III. Early Latin writings tell of a Christian warrior named Arturius (Arthur, in English) who led the British citizens to defeat these barbarian invades, and brought an extended period of peace to the lands of Britain.
IV. Long ago, the British Isles were part of the far-flung Roman Empire that extended across most of Europe and into Africa and Asia.
V. The romantic legend of King Arthur and his knights of the Round Table, one of the most popular and widespread stories of all time, appears to have some foundation in history.

The BEST order is:
A. V, IV, III, II, I B. V, IV, II, I, III C. IV, V, II, III, I D. IV, III, II, I, V

20. I. The cylinder was allowed to cool until it could stand on its own, and then it was cut from the tube and split down the side with a single straight cut. 20.____
II. Nineteenth-century glassmakers, who had not yet discovered the glazier's modern techniques for making panes of glass, had to create a method for converting their blown gas into flat sheets.
III. The bubble was then pierced at the end to make a hole that opened up while the glassmaker gently spun it, creating a cylinder of glass.
IV. Turned on its side and laid on a conveyor belt, the cylinder was strengthened, or tempered, by being heated again and cooled very slowly, eventually flattening out into a single rectangular of glass.
V. To do this, the glassmaker dipped the end of a long tube into melted glass and blew into the other end of the tube, creating an expanding bubble of glass.

The BEST order is:
A. II, V, III, IV, I B. II, IV, V, III, I C. III, V, II, IV, I D. III, I, IV, V, II

21. I. The splints are almost always hidden, but horses are occasionally born whose splinted toes project from the leg on either side, just above the hoof. 21.____
II. The second and fourth toes remained, but shrank to thin splints of bone that fused invisibly to the horse's leg bone.
III. Horses are unique among mammals, having evolved feet that each end in what is essentially a single toe, capped by a large, sturdy hoof.
IV. Julius Caesar, an emperor of ancient Rome, was said to have owned one of these three-toed horses, and considered it so special that he would not permit anyone else to ride it.
V. Though the horse's earlier ancestors possessed the traditional mammalian set of five toes on each foot, the horse has retained only its third toe; its first and fifth toes disappeared completely as the horse evolved.

The BEST order is:
A. III, V, II, I, IV B. V, III, II, IV, I C. III, II, V, I, IV D. V, II, III, I, IV

22. I. The new building materials—some of which are twenty feet long, and weigh nearly six tons—were transported to Pohnpei on rafts, and were brought into their present position by using hibiscus fiber ropes and leverage to move the stone columns upward along the inclined trunks of coconut palm trees. 22.____
II. The ancestors built great fires to heat the stone, and then poured cool seawater on the columns, which caused the stone to contract and split along natural fracture lines.
III. The now-abandoned enclave of Nan Madol, a group of 92 man-made islands off the shore of the Micronesian island of Pohnpei, is estimated to have been built around the year 500 A.D.
IV. The islanders say their ancestors quarried stone columns from a nearby island, where large basalt columns were formed by the cooling of molten lava.
V. The structures of Nan Madol are remarkable for the sheer size of some of the stone "longs" or columns that were used to create the walls of the offshore community, and today anthropologists can only rely on the information of existing local people for clues about how Nan Madol was built.

The BEST order is:
A. V, IV, III, II, I B. V, III, I, IV, II C. III, V, IV, II, I D. III, I, IV, II, V

23. I. One of the most easily manipulated substances on earth, glass can be made into ceramic tiles that are composed of over 90% air. 22.____
II. NASA's space shuttles are the first spacecraft ever designed to leave and re-enter the earth's atmosphere while remaining intact.
III. These ceramic tiles are such effective insulators that when a tile emerges from the oven in which it was fired, it can be held safely in a person's hand by the edges while its interior still glows at a temperature well over 2000ºF.
IV. Eventually, the engineers were led to a material that is as old as our most ancient civilization.
V. Because the temperature during atmospheric re-entry is so incredibly hot, it took NASA's engineers some time to find a substance capable of protecting the shuttles.

The BEST order is:
A. V, II, I, II, IV B. II, V, IV, I, III C. II, III, I, IV, V D. V, IV, III, I, II

24. I. The secret to teaching any parakeet to talk is patience, and the understanding that when a bird talks," it is simply imitating what it hears, rather than putting ideas into words. 24.____
II. You should stay just out of sight of the bird and repeat the phrase you want it to learn, for at least fifteen minutes every morning and evening.
III. It is important to leave the bird without any words of encouragement or farewell; otherwise it might combine stray remarks or phrases, such as "Good night," with the phrase you are trying to teach it.
IV. For this reason, to train your bird to imitate your words you should keep it free of any distractions, especially other noises, while you are giving it "lesson."
V. After your repetition, you should quietly leave the bird alone for a while, to think over what it has just heard.
The BEST order is:
A. I, IV, II, V, III B. I, II, IV, III, V C. III, II, I, V, IV D. III, I, V, IV, II

25. I. As a school approaches, fishermen from neighboring communities join their fishing boats together as a fleet, and string their gill nets together to make a huge fence that is held up by cork floats. 25.____
II. At a signal from the party leaders, or *nakura*, the family members pound the sides of the boats or beat the water with long poles, creating a sudden and deafening noise.
III. The fishermen work together to drag the trap into a half-circle that may reach 300 yards in diameter, and then the families move their boats to form the other half of the circle around the school of fish.
IV. The school of fish flee from the commotion into the awaiting trap, where a final wall of net is thrown over the open end of the half-circle, securing the day's haul.
V. Indonesian people from the area around the Sulu islands live on the sea, in floating villages made of lashed-together or stilted homes, and make much of their living by fishing their home waters for migrating schools of snapper, scad, and other fish.
The BEST order is:
A. I, V, III, IV, II B. I, II, IV, III, V C. V, I, II, III, IV D. V, I, III, II, IV

KEY (CORRECT ANSWERS)

1.	D	11.	C
2.	D	12.	A
3.	B	13.	D
4.	A	14.	C
5.	C	15.	D
6.	C	16.	C
7.	D	17.	A
8.	D	18.	D
9.	A	19.	B
10.	B	20.	A

21. A
22. C
23. B
24. A
25. D

**PHILOSOPHY, PRINCIPLES, PRACTICES, AND TECHNICS
OF
SUPERVISION, ADMINISTRATION, MANAGEMENT, AND ORGANIZATION**

TABLE OF CONTENTS

PHILOSOPHY, PRINCIPLES, PRACTICES, AND TECHNICS
OF
SUPERVISION, ADMINISTRATION, MANAGEMENT, AND ORGANIZATION

MEANING OF SUPERVISION

The extension of the democratic philosophy has been accompanied by an extension in the scope of supervision. Modern leaders and supervisors no longer think of supervision in the narrow sense of being confined chiefly to visiting employees, supplying materials, or rating the staff. They regard supervision as being intimately related to all the concerned agencies of society, they speak of the supervisor's function in terms of "growth," rather than the "improvement" of employees.

This modern concept of supervision may be defined as follows: Supervision is leadership and the development of leadership within groups which are cooperatively engaged in inspection, research, training, guidance, and evaluation.

THE OLD AND THE NEW SUPERVISION

TRADITIONAL
1. Inspection
2. Focused on the employee
3. Visitation
4. Random and haphazard
5. Imposed and authoritarian
6. One person usually

MODERN
1. Study and analysis
2. Focused on aims, materials, methods, supervisors, employees, environment
3. Demonstrations, intervisitation, workshops, directed reading, bulletins, etc.
4. Definitely organized and planned (scientific)
5. Cooperative and democratic
6. Many persons involved (creative)

THE EIGHT (8) BASIC PRINCIPLES OF THE NEW SUPERVISION

I. Principle of Responsibility
Authority to act and responsibility for acting must be joined.
   A. If you give responsibility, give authority.
   B. Define employee duties clearly.
   C. Protect employees from criticism by others.
   D. Recognize the rights as well as obligations of employees.
   E. Achieve the aims of a democratic society insofar as it is possible within the area of your work.
   F. Establish a situation favorable to training and learning.
   G. Accept ultimate responsibility for everything done in your section, unit, office, division, department.
   H. Good administration and good supervision are inseparable.

II. Principle of Authority
The success of the supervisor is measured by the extent to which the power of authority is not used.
   A. Exercise simplicity and informality in supervision
   B. Use the simplest machinery of supervision
   C. If it is good for the organization as a whole, it is probably justified.
   D. Seldom be arbitrary or authoritative.
   E. Do not base your work on the power of position or of personality.
   F. Permit and encourage the free expression of opinions.

III. Principle of Self-Growth
The success of the supervisor is measured by the extent to which, and the speed with which, he is no longer needed.
   A. Base criticism on principles, not on specifics.
   B. Point out higher activities to employees.
   C. Train for self-thinking by employees to meet new situations.
   D. Stimulate initiative, self-reliance, and individual responsibility
   E. Concentrate on stimulating the growth of employees rather than on removing defects.

IV. Principle of Individual Worth
Respect for the individual is a paramount consideration in supervision.
   A. Be human and sympathetic in dealing with employees.
   B. Don't nag about things to be done.
   C. Recognize the individual differences among employees and seek opportunities to permit best expression of each personality.

V. Principle of Creative Leadership
The best supervision is that which is not apparent to the employee.
   A. Stimulate, don't drive employees to creative action.
   B. Emphasize doing good things.
   C. Encourage employees to do what they do best.
   D. Do not be too greatly concerned with details of subject or method.
   E. Do not be concerned exclusively with immediate problems and activities.
   F. Reveal higher activities and make them both desired and maximally possible.
   G. Determine procedures in the light of each situation but see that these are derived from a sound basic philosophy.
   H. Aid, inspire, and lead so as to liberate the creative spirit latent in all good employees.

VI. Principle of Success and Failure
There are no unsuccessful employees, only unsuccessful supervisors who have failed to give proper leadership.
   A. Adapt suggestions to the capacities, attitudes, and prejudices of employees.
   B. Be gradual, be progressive, be persistent.
   C. Help the employee find the general principle; have the employee apply his own problem to the general principle.
   D. Give adequate appreciation for good work and honest effort.
   E. Anticipate employee difficulties and help to prevent them.
   F. Encourage employees to do the desirable things they will do anyway.
   G. Judge your supervision by the results it secures.

VII. Principle of Science
Successful supervision is scientific, objective, and experimental. It is based on facts, not on prejudices.
A. Be cumulative in results.
B. Never divorce your suggestions from the goals of training.
C. Don't be impatient of results.
D. Keep all matters on a professional, not a personal, level.
E. Do not be concerned exclusively with immediate problems and activities.
F. Use objective means of determining achievement and rating where possible.

VIII. Principle of Cooperation
Supervision is a cooperative enterprise between supervisor and employee.
A. Begin with conditions as they are.
B. Ask opinions of all involved when formulating policies.
C. Organization is as good as its weakest link.
D. Let employees help to determine policies and department programs.
E. Be approachable and accessible—physically and mentally.
F. Develop pleasant social relationships.

WHAT IS ADMINISTRATION

Administration is concerned with providing the environment, the material facilities, and the operational procedures that will promote the maximum growth and development of supervisors and employees. (Organization is an aspect and a concomitant of administration.)

There is no sharp line of demarcation between supervision and administration; these functions are intimately interrelated and, often, overlapping. They are complementary activities.

I. Practices Commonly Classed as "Supervisory"
A. Conducting employees' conferences
B. Visiting sections, units, offices, divisions, departments
C. Arranging for demonstrations
D. Examining plans
E. Suggesting professional reading
F. Interpreting bulletins
G. Recommending in-service training courses
H. Encouraging experimentation
I. Appraising employee morale
J. Providing for intervisitation

II. Practices Commonly Classified as "Administrative"
A. Management of the office
B. Arrangement of schedules for extra duties
C. Assignment of rooms or areas
D. Distribution of supplies
E. Keeping records and reports
F. Care of audio-visual materials
G. Keeping inventory records
H. Checking record cards and books

I. Programming special activities
J. Checking on the attendance and punctuality of employees

III. Practices Commonly Classified as Both "Supervisory" and "Administrative"
A. Program construction
B. Testing or evaluating outcomes
C. Personnel accounting
D. Ordering instructional materials

RESPONSIBILITIES OF THE SUPERVISOR

A person employed in a supervisory capacity must constantly be able to improve his own efficiency and ability. He represent the employer to the employees and only continuous self-examination can make him a capable supervisor.

Leadership and training are the supervisor's responsibility. An efficient working unit is one in which the employees work with the supervisor. It is his job to bring out the best in his employees. He must always be relaxed, courteous, and calm in his association with his employees. Their feelings are important, and a harsh attitude does not develop the most efficient employees.

COMPETENCES OF THE SUPERVISOR

I. Complete knowledge of the duties and responsibilities of his position.
II. To be able to organize a job, plan ahead, and carry through.
III. To have self-confidence and initiative.
IV. To be able to handle the unexpected situation and make quick decisions.
V. To be able to properly train subordinates in the positions they are best suited for.
VI. To be able to keep good human relations among his subordinates.
VII. To be able to keep good human relations between his subordinates and himself and to earn their respect and trust.

THE PROFESSIONAL SUPERVISOR-EMPLOYEE RELATIONSHIP

There are two kinds of efficiency: one kind is only apparent and is produced in organizations through the exercise of mere discipline; this is but a simulation of the second, or true, efficiency which springs from spontaneous cooperation. If you are a manager, no matter how great or small your responsibility, it is your job, in the final analysis, to create and develop this involuntary cooperation among the people whom you supervise. For, no matter how powerful a combination of money, machines, and materials a company may have, this is a dead and sterile thing without a team of willing, thinking, and articulate people to guide it.

The following 21 points are presented as indicative of the exemplary basic relationship that should exist between supervisor and employee:

1. Each person wants to be liked and respected by his fellow employee and wants to be treated with consideration and respect by his superior.
2. The most competent employee will make an error. However, in a unit where good relations exist between the supervisor and his employees, tenseness and fear do not exist. Thus, errors are not hidden or covered up, and the efficiency of a unit is not impaired.

3. Subordinates resent rules, regulations, or orders that are unreasonable or unexplained.
4. Subordinates are quick to resent unfairness, harshness, injustices, and favoritism.
5. An employee will accept responsibility if he knows that he will be complimented for a job well done, and not too harshly chastised for failure; that his supervisor will check the cause of the failure, and, if it was the supervisor's fault, he will assume the blame therefore. If it was the employee's fault, his supervisor will explain the correct method or means of handling the responsibility.
6. An employee wants to receive credit for a suggestion he has made, that is used. If a suggestion cannot be used, the employee is entitled to an explanation. The supervisor should not say "no" and close the subject.
7. Fear and worry slow up a worker's ability. Poor working environment can impair his physical and mental health. A good supervisor avoids forceful methods, threats, and arguments to get a job done.
8. A forceful supervisor is able to train his employees individually and as a team, and is able to motivate them in the proper channels.
9. A mature supervisor is able to properly evaluate his subordinates and to keep them happy and satisfied.
10. A sensitive supervisor will never patronize his subordinates.
11. A worthy supervisor will respect his employees' confidences.
12. Definite and clear-cut responsibilities should be assigned to each executive.
13. Responsibility should always be coupled with corresponding authority.
14. No change should be made in the scope or responsibilities of a position without a definite understanding to that effect on the part of all persons concerned.
15. No executive or employee, occupying a single position in the organization, should be subject to definite orders from more than one source.
16. Orders should never be given to subordinates over the head of a responsible executive. Rather than do this, the officer in question should be supplanted.
17. Criticisms of subordinates should, whoever possible, be made privately, and in no case should a subordinate be criticized in the presence of executives or employees of equal or lower rank.
18. No dispute or difference between executives or employees as to authority or responsibilities should be considered too trivial for prompt and careful adjudication.
19. Promotions, wage changes, and disciplinary action should always be approved by the executive immediately superior to the one directly responsible.
20. No executive or employee should ever be required, or expected, to be at the same time an assistant to, and critic of, another.
21. Any executive whose work is subject to regular inspection should, wherever practicable, be given the assistance and facilities necessary to enable him to maintain an independent check of the quality of his work.

MINI-TEXT IN SUPERVISION, ADMINISTRATION, MANAGEMENT, AND ORGANIZATION

I. Brief Highlights

Listed concisely and sequentially are major headings and important data in the field for quick recall and review.

A. Levels of Management

Any organization of some size has several levels of management. In terms of a ladder, the levels are:

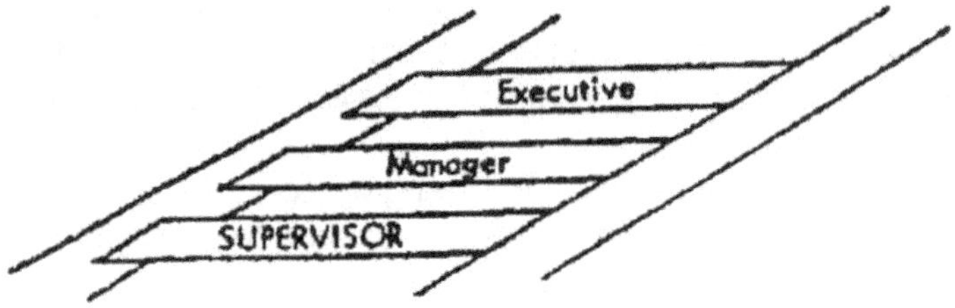

The first level is very important because it is the beginning point of management leadership.

B. What the Supervisor Must Learn

A supervisor must learn to:

1. Deal with people and their differences
2. Get the job done through people
3. Recognize the problems when they exist
4. Overcome obstacles to good performance
5. Evaluate the performance of people
6. Check his own performance in terms of accomplishment

C. A Definition of Supervisor

The term supervisor means any individual having authority, in the interests of the employer, to hire, transfer, suspend, lay-off, recall, promote, discharge, assign, reward, or discipline other employees or responsibility to direct them, or to adjust their grievances, or effectively to recommend such action, if, in connection with the foregoing, exercise of such authority is not of a merely routine or clerical nature but requires the use of independent judgment.

D. Elements of the Team Concept

What is involved in teamwork? The component parts are:

1. Members
2. A leader
3. Goals
4. Plans
5. Cooperation
6. Spirit

E. Principles of Organization

1. A team member must know what his job is.
2. Be sure that the nature and scope of a job are understood.
3. Authority and responsibility should be carefully spelled out.
4. A supervisor should be permitted to make the maximum number of decisions affecting his employees.
5. Employees should report to only one supervisor.
6. A supervisor should direct only as many employees as he can handle effectively.
7. An organization plan should be flexible.

8. Inspection and performance of work should be separate.
9. Organizational problems should receive immediate attention.
10. Assign work in line with ability and experience.

F. The Four Important Parts of Every Job
1. Inherent in every job is the *accountability* for results.
2. A second set of factors in every job is *responsibilities*.
3. Along with duties and responsibilities one must have the *authority* to act within certain limits without obtaining permission to proceed.
4. No job exists in a vacuum. The supervisor is surrounded by key *relationships*.

G. Principles of Delegation
Where work is delegated for the first time, the supervisor should think in terms of these questions:
1. Who is best qualified to do this?
2. Can an employee improve his abilities by doing this?
3. How long should an employee spend on this?
4. Are there any special problems for which he will need guidance?
5. How broad a delegation can I make?

H. Principles of Effective Communications
1. Determine the media.
2. To whom directed?
3. Identification and source authority.
4. Is communication understood?

I. Principles of Work Improvement
1. Most people usually do only the work which is assigned to them.
2. Workers are likely to fit assigned work into the time available to perform it.
3. A good workload usually stimulates output.
4. People usually do their best work when they know that results will be reviewed or inspected.
5. Employees usually feel that someone else is responsible for conditions of work, workplace layout, job methods, type of tools/equipment, and other such factors.
6. Employees are usually defensive about their job security.
7. Employees have natural resistance to change.
8. Employees can support or destroy a supervisor.
9. A supervisor usually earns the respect of his people through his personal example of diligence and efficiency.

J. Areas of Job Improvement
The areas of job improvement are quite numerous, but the most common ones which a supervisor can identify and utilize are:
1. Departmental layout
2. Flow of work
3. Workplace layout
4. Utilization of manpower
5. Work methods
6. Materials handling

7. Utilization
8. Motion economy

K. Seven Key Points in Making Improvements
1. Select the job to be improved
2. Study how it is being done now
3. Question the present method
4. Determine actions to be taken
5. Chart proposed method
6. Get approval and apply
7. Solicit worker participation

I. Corrective Techniques of Job Improvement
Specific Problems
1. Size of workload
2. Inability to meet schedules
3. Strain and fatigue
4. Improper use of men and skills
5. Waste, poor quality, unsafe conditions
6. Bottleneck conditions that hinder output
7. Poor utilization of equipment and machine
8. Efficiency and productivity of labor

General Improvement
1. Departmental layout
2. Flow of work
3. Work plan layout
4. Utilization of manpower
5. Work methods
6. Materials handling
7. Utilization of equipment
8. Motion economy

Corrective Techniques
1. Study with scale model
2. Flow chart study
3. Motion analysis
4. Comparison of units produced to standard allowance
5. Methods analysis
6. Flow chart and equipment study
7. Down time vs. running time
8. Motion analysis

M. A Planning Checklist
1. Objectives
2. Controls
3. Delegations
4. Communications
5. Resources
6. Manpower

7. Equipment
8. Supplies and materials
9. Utilization of time
10. Safety
11. Money
12. Work
13. Timing of improvements

N. Five Characteristics of Good Directions

In order to get results, directions must be:

1. Possible of accomplishment
2. Agreeable with worker interests
3. Related to mission
4. Planned and complete
5. Unmistakably clear

O. Types of Directions

1. Demands or direct orders
2. Requests
3. Suggestion or implication
4. volunteering

P. Controls

A typical listing of the overall areas in which the supervisor should establish controls might be:

1. Manpower
2. Materials
3. Quality of work
4. Quantity of work
5. Time
6. Space
7. Money
8. Methods

Q. Orienting the New Employee

1. Prepare for him
2. Welcome the new employee
3. Orientation for the job
4. Follow-up

R. Checklist for Orienting New Employees

	Yes	No
1. Do you appreciate the feelings of new employees when they first report for work?	___	___
2. Are you aware of the fact that the new employee must make a big adjustment to his job?	___	___
3. Have you given him good reasons for liking the job and the organization?	___	___
4. Have you prepared for his first day on the job?	___	___
5. Did you welcome him cordially and make him feel needed?	___	___

	Yes	No
6. Did you establish rapport with him so that he feels free to talk and discuss matters with you?	___	___
7. Did you explain his job to him and his relationship to you?	___	___
8. Does he know that his work will be evaluated periodically on a basis that is fair and objective?	___	___
9. Did you introduce him to his fellow workers in such a way that they are likely to accept him?	___	___
10. Does he know what employee benefits he will receive?	___	___
11. Does he understand the importance of being on the job and what to do if he must leave his duty station?	___	___
12. Has he been impressed with the importance of accident prevention and safe practice?	___	___
13. Does he generally know his way around the department?	___	___
14. Is he under the guidance of a sponsor who will teach the right way of doing things?	___	___
15. Do you plan to follow-up so that he will continue to adjust successfully to his job?	___	___

S. Principles of Learning
1. Motivation
2. Demonstration or explanation
3. Practice

T. Causes of Poor Performance
1. Improper training for job
2. Wrong tools
3. Inadequate directions
4. Lack of supervisory follow-up
5. Poor communications
6. Lack of standards of performance
7. Wrong work habits
8. Low morale
9. Other

U. Four Major Steps in On-The-Job Instruction
1. Prepare the worker
2. Present the operation
3. Tryout performance
4. Follow-up

V. Employees Want Five Things
1. Security
2. Opportunity
3. Recognition
4. Inclusion
5. Expression

W. Some Don'ts in Regard to Praise
1. Don't praise a person for something he hasn't done.
2. Don't praise a person unless you can be sincere.
3. Don't be sparing in praise just because your superior withholds it from you.
4. Don't let too much time elapse between good performance and recognition of it

X. How to Gain Your Workers' Confidence
Methods of developing confidence include such things as:
1. Knowing the interests, habits, hobbies of employees
2. Admitting your own inadequacies
3. Sharing and telling of confidence in others
4. Supporting people when they are in trouble
5. Delegating matters that can be well handled
6. Being frank and straightforward about problems and working conditions
7. Encouraging others to bring their problems to you
8. Taking action on problems which impede worker progress

Y. Sources of Employee Problems
On-the-job causes might be such things as:
1. A feeling that favoritism is exercised in assignments
2. Assignment of overtime
3. An undue amount of supervision
4. Changing methods or systems
5. Stealing of ideas or trade secrets
6. Lack of interest in job
7. Threat of reduction in force
8. Ignorance or lack of communications
9. Poor equipment
10. Lack of knowing how supervisor feels toward employee
11. Shift assignments

Off-the-job problems might have to do with:
1. Health
2. Finances
3. Housing
4. Family

Z. The Supervisor's Key to Discipline
There are several key points about discipline which the supervisor should keep in mind:
1. Job discipline is one of the disciplines of life and is directed by the supervisor.
2. It is more important to correct an employee fault than to fix blame for it.
3. Employee performance is affected by problems both on the job and off.
4. Sudden or abrupt changes in behavior can be indications of important employee problems.
5. Problems should be dealt with as soon as possible after they are identified.
6. The attitude of the supervisor may have more to do with solving problems than the techniques of problem solving.
7. Correction of employee behavior should be resorted to only after the supervisor is sure that training or counseling will not be helpful.

8. Be sure to document your disciplinary actions.
9. Make sure that you are disciplining on the basis of facts rather than personal feelings.
10. Take each disciplinary step in order, being careful not to make snap judgments, or decisions based on impatience.

AA. Five Important Processes of Management
1. Planning
2. Organizing
3. Scheduling
4. Controlling
5. Motivating

BB. When the Supervisor Fails to Plan
1. Supervisor creates impression of not knowing his job
2. May lead to excessive overtime
3. Job runs itself—supervisor lacks control
4. Deadlines and appointments missed
5. Parts of the work go undone
6. Work interrupted by emergencies
7. Sets a bad example
8. Uneven workload creates peaks and valleys
9. Too much time on minor details at expense of more important tasks

CC. Fourteen General Principles of Management
1. Division of work
2. Authority and responsibility
3. Discipline
4. Unity of command
5. Unity of direction
6. Subordination of individual interest to general interest
7. Remuneration of personnel
8. Centralization
9. Scalar chain
10. Order
11. Equity
12. Stability of tenure of personnel
13. Initiative
14. Esprit de corps

DD. Change

Bringing about change is perhaps attempted more often, and yet less well understood, than anything else the supervisor does. How do people generally react to change? (People tend to resist change that is imposed upon them by other individuals or circumstances.

Change is characteristic of every situation. It is a part of every real endeavor where the efforts of people are concerned.

1. Why do people resist change?
   People may resist change because of:
   a. Fear of the unknown
   b. Implied criticism
   c. Unpleasant experiences in the past
   d. Fear of loss of status
   e. Threat to the ego
   f. Fear of loss of economic stability

2. How can we best overcome the resistance to change?
   In initiating change, take these steps:
   a. Get ready to sell
   b. Identify sources of help
   c. Anticipate objections
   d. Sell benefits
   e. Listen in depth
   f. Follow up

II. Brief Topical Summaries

A. Who/What is the Supervisor?
   1. The supervisor is often called the "highest level employee and the lowest level manager."
   2. A supervisor is a member of both management and the work group. He acts as a bridge between the two.
   3. Most problems in supervision are in the area of human relations, or people problems.
   4. Employees expect: Respect, opportunity to learn and to advance, and a sense of belonging, and so forth.
   5. Supervisors are responsible for directing people and organizing work. Planning is of paramount importance.
   6. A position description is a set of duties and responsibilities inherent to a given position.
   7. It is important to keep the position description up-to-date and to provide each employee with his own copy.

B. The Sociology of Work
   1. People are alike in many ways; however, each individual is unique.
   2. The supervisor is challenged in getting to know employee differences. Acquiring skills in evaluating individuals is an asset.
   3. Maintaining meaningful working relationships in the organization is of great importance.
   4. The supervisor has an obligation to help individuals to develop to their fullest potential.
   5. Job rotation on a planned basis helps to build versatility and to maintain interest and enthusiasm in work groups.
   6. Cross training (job rotation) provides backup skills.

7. The supervisor can help reduce tension by maintaining a sense of humor, providing guidance to employees, and by making reasonable and timely decisions. Employees respond favorably to working under reasonably predictable circumstances.
8. Change is characteristic of all managerial behavior. The supervisor must adjust to changes in procedures, new methods, technological changes, and to a number of new and sometimes challenging situations.
9. To overcome the natural tendency for people to resist change, the supervisor should become more skillful in initiating change.

C. Principles and Practices of Supervision

1. Employees should be required to answer to only one superior.
2. A supervisor can effectively direct only a limited number of employees, depending upon the complexity, variety, and proximity of the jobs involved.
3. The organizational chart presents the organization in graphic form. It reflects lines of authority and responsibility as well as interrelationships of units within the organization.
4. Distribution of work can be improved through an analysis using the "Work Distribution Chart."
5. The "Work Distribution Chart" reflects the division of work within a unit in understandable form.
6. When related tasks are given to an employee, he has a better chance of increasing his skills through training.
7. The individual who is given the responsibility for tasks must also be given the appropriate authority to insure adequate results.
8. The supervisor should delegate repetitive, routine work. Preparation of recurring reports, maintaining leave and attendance records are some examples.
9. Good discipline is essential to good task performance. Discipline is reflected in the actions of employees on the job in the absence of supervision.
10. Disciplinary action may have to be taken when the positive aspects of discipline have failed. Reprimand, warning, and suspension are examples of disciplinary action.
11. If a situation calls for a reprimand, be sure it is deserved and remember it is to be done in private.

D. Dynamic Leadership

1. A style is a personal method or manner of exerting influence.
2. Authoritarian leaders often see themselves as the source of power and authority.
3. The democratic leader often perceives the group as the source of authority and power.
4. Supervisors tend to do better when using the pattern of leadership that is most natural for them.
5. Social scientists suggest that the effective supervisor use the leadership style that best fits the problem or circumstances involved.
6. All four styles—telling, selling, consulting, joining—have their place. Using one does not preclude using the other at another time.

7. The theory X point of view assumes that the average person dislikes work, will avoid it whenever possible, and must be coerced to achieve organizational objectives.
8. The theory Y point of view assumes that the average person considers work to be a natural as play, and, when the individual is committed, he requires little supervision or direction to accomplish desired objectives.
9. The leader's basic assumptions concerning human behavior and human nature affect his actions, decisions, and other managerial practices.
10. Dissatisfaction among employees is often present, but difficult to isolate. The supervisor should seek to weaken dissatisfaction by keeping promises, being sincere and considerate, keeping employees informed, and so forth.
11. Constructive suggestions should be encouraged during the natural progress of the work.

E. Processes for Solving Problems

1. People find their daily tasks more meaningful and satisfying when they can improve them.
2. The causes of problems, or the key factors, are often hidden in the background. Ability to solve problems often involves the ability to isolate them from their backgrounds. There is some substance to the cliché that some persons "can't see the forest for the trees."
3. New procedures are often developed from old ones. Problems should be broken down into manageable parts. New ideas can be adapted from old one.
4. People think differently in problem-solving situations. Using a logical, patterned approach is often useful. One approach found to be useful includes these steps:
    a. Define the problem
    b. Establish objectives
    c. Get the facts
    d. Weigh and decide
    e. Take action
    f. Evaluate action

F. Training for Results

1. Participants respond best when they feel training is important to them.
2. The supervisor has responsibility for the training and development of those who report to him.
3. When training is delegated to others, great care must be exercised to insure the trainer has knowledge, aptitude, and interest for his work as a trainer.
4. Training (learning) of some type goes on continually. The most successful supervisor makes certain the learning contributes in a productive manner to operational goals.
5. New employees are particularly susceptible to training. Older employees facing new job situations require specific training, as well as having need for development and growth opportunities.
6. Training needs require continuous monitoring.
7. The training officer of an agency is a professional with a responsibility to assist supervisors in solving training problems.

8. Many of the self-development steps important to the supervisor's own growth are equally important to the development of peers and subordinates. Knowledge of these is important when the supervisor consults with others on development and growth opportunities.

G. Health, Safety, and Accident Prevention
  1. Management-minded supervisors take appropriate measures to assist employees in maintaining health and in assuring safe practices in the work environment.
  2. Effective safety training and practices help to avoid injury and accidents.
  3. Safety should be a management goal. All infractions of safety which are observed should be corrected without exception.
  4. Employees' safety attitude, training and instruction, provision of safe tools and equipment, supervision, and leadership are considered highly important factors which contribute to safety and which can be influenced directly by supervisors.
  5. When accidents do occur, they should be investigated promptly for very important reasons, including the fact that information which is gained can be used to prevent accidents in the future.

H. Equal Employment Opportunity
  1. The supervisor should endeavor to treat all employees fairly, without regard to religion, race, sex, or national origin.
  2. Groups tend to reflect the attitude of the leader. Prejudice can be detected even in very subtle form. Supervisors must strive to create a feeling of mutual respect and confidence in every employee.
  3. Complete utilization of all human resources is a national goal. Equitable consideration should be accorded women in the work force, minority-group members, the physically and mentally handicapped, and the older employee. The important question is: "Who can do the job?"
  4. Training opportunities, recognition for performance, overtime assignments, promotional opportunities, and all other personnel actions are to be handled on an equitable basis.

I. Improving Communications
  1. Communications is achieving understanding between the sender and the receiver of a message. It also means sharing information—the creation of understanding.
  2. Communication is basic to all human activity. Words are means of conveying meanings; however, real meanings are in people.
  3. There are very practical differences in the effectiveness of one-way, impersonal, and two-way communications. Words spoken face-to-face are better understood. Telephone conversations are effective, but lack the rapport of person-to-person exchanges. The whole person communicates.
  4. Cooperation and communication in an organization go hand in hand. When there is a mutual respect between people, spelling out rules and procedures for communicating is unnecessary.
  5. There are several barriers to effective communications. These include failure to listen with respect and understanding, lack of skill in feedback, and misinterpreting the meanings of words used by the speaker. It is also common

practice to listen to what we want to hear, and tune out things we do not want to hear.

6. Communication is management's chief problem. The supervisor should accept the challenge to communicate more effectively and to improve interagency and intra-agency communications.
7. The supervisor may often plan for and conduct meetings. The planning phase is critical and may determine the success or the failure of a meeting.
8. Speaking before groups usually requires extra effort. Stage fright may never disappear completely, but it can be controlled.

J. Self-Development

1. Every employee is responsible for his own self-development.
2. Toastmaster and toastmistress clubs offer opportunities to improve skills in oral communications.
3. Planning for one's own self-development is of vital importance. Supervisors know their own strengths and limitations better than anyone else.
4. Many opportunities are open to aid the supervisor in his developmental efforts, including job assignments; training opportunities, both governmental and non-governmental—to include universities and professional conferences and seminars.
5. Programmed instruction offers a means of studying at one's own rate.
6. Where difficulties may arise from a supervisor's being away from his work for training, he may participate in televised home study or correspondence courses to meet his self-development needs.

K. Teaching and Training

1. The Teaching Process

Teaching is encouraging and guiding the learning activities of students toward established goals. In most cases this process consists of five steps: preparation, presentation, summarization, evaluation, and application.

a. Preparation

Preparation is two-fold in nature; that of the supervisor and the employee. Preparation by the supervisor is absolutely essential to success. He must know what, when, where, how, and whom he will teach. Some of the factors that should be considered are:

1) The objectives
2) The materials needed
3) The methods to be used
4) Employee participation
5) Employee interest
6) Training aids
7) Evaluation
8) Summarization

Employee preparation consists in preparing the employee to receive the material. Probably the most important single factor in the preparation of the employee is arousing and maintaining his interest. He must know the objectives of the training, why he is there, how the material can be used, and its importance to him.

b. Presentation
In presentation, have a carefully designed plan and follow it. The plan should be accurate and complete, yet flexible enough to meet situations as they arise. The method of presentation will be determined by the particular situation and objectives.

c. Summary
A summary should be made at the end of every training unit and program. In addition, there may be internal summaries depending on the nature of the material being taught. The important thing is that the trainee must always be able to understand how each part of the new material relates to the whole.

d. Application
The supervisor must arrange work so the employee will be given a chance to apply new knowledge or skills while the material is still clear in his mind and interest is high. The trainee does not really know whether he has learned the material until he has been given a chance to apply it. If the material is not applied, it loses most of its value.

e. Evaluation
The purpose of all training is to promote learning. To determine whether the training has been a success or failure, the supervisor must evaluate this learning.
In the broadest sense, evaluation includes all the devices, methods, skills, and techniques used by the supervisor to keep himself and the employees informed as to their progress toward the objectives they are pursuing. The extent to which the employee has mastered the knowledge, skills, and abilities, or changed his attitudes, as determined by the program objectives, is the extent to which instruction has succeeded or failed.
Evaluation should not be confined to the end of the lesson, day, or program but should be used continuously. We shall note later the way this relates to the rest of the teaching process.

2. Teaching Methods
A teaching method is a pattern of identifiable student and instructor activity used in presenting training material.
All supervisors are faced with the problem of deciding which method should be used at a given time.

a. Lecture
The lecture is direct oral presentation of material by the supervisor. The present trend is to place less emphasis on the trainer's activity and more on that of the trainee.

b. Discussion
Teaching by discussion or conference involves using questions and other techniques to arouse interest and focus attention upon certain areas, and by doing so creating a learning situation. This can be one of the most

valuable methods because it gives the employees an opportunity to express their ideas and pool their knowledge.

c. Demonstration
The demonstration is used to teach how something works or how to do something. It can be used to show a principle or what the results of a series of actions will be. A well-staged demonstration is particularly effective because it shows proper methods of performance in a realistic manner.

d. Performance
Performance is one of the most fundamental of all learning techniques or teaching methods. The trainee may be able to tell how a specific operation should be performed but he cannot be sure he knows how to perform the operation until he has done so.
As with all methods, there are certain advantages and disadvantages to each method.

e. Which Method to Use
Moreover, there are other methods and techniques of teaching. It is difficult to use any method without other methods entering into it. In any learning situation, a combination of methods is usually more effective than any one method alone.

Finally, evaluation must be integrated into the other aspects of the teaching-learning process.

It must be used in the motivation of the trainees; it must be used to assist in developing understanding during the training; and it must be related to employee application of the results of training.

This is distinctly the role of the supervisor.

www.ingramcontent.com/pod-product-compliance
Lightning Source LLC
Chambersburg PA
CBHW081815300426
44116CB00014B/2371